ANNALS OF COMMUNISM

Each volume in the series Annals of Communism will publish selected
and previously inaccessible documents from former Soviet state and
party archives in a narrative that develops a particular topic in the
history of Soviet and international communism. Separate English and
Russian editions will be prepared. Russian and Western scholars work
together to prepare the documents for each volume. Documents are
chosen not for their support of any single interpretation but for their
particular historical importance or their general value in deepening
understanding and facilitating discussion. The volumes are designed to
be useful to students, scholars, and interested general readers.

Gulag Voices

An Anthology

Edited by Anne Applebaum

Yale UNIVERSITY PRESS

New Haven & London

Yale University Press books may be purchased in quantity for educational,
business, or promotional use. For information, please e-mail sales.press@yale.edu
(U.S. office) or sales@yaleup.co.uk (U.K. office).

Designed by James J. Johnson and set in Sabon Roman type by Westchester Book Group.
Printed in the United States of America.

Library of Congress Cataloging-in-Publication Data

Gulag voices : an anthology / edited by Anne Applebaum.
    p. cm. — (Annals of communism)
    ISBN 978-0-300-15320-0 (alk. paper)
    1. Soviet Union—History—1925–1953—Biography.   2. Soviet Union—History—
1953–1985—Biography.   3. Prisoners—Soviet Union—Biography.   4. Political
prisoners—Soviet Union—Biography.   5. Glavnoe upravlenie ispravitel'no-trudovykh
lagereĭ OGPU—History.   6. Prisoners—Soviet Union—Social conditions.   7. Political
prisoners—Soviet Union—Social conditions.   8. Forced labor—Soviet Union—
History.   9. Concentration camps—Soviet Union—History.   I. Applebaum, Anne, 1964–

    DK268.A1G84 2011
    365'.45092247—dc22

                                                                2010033711

A catalogue record for this book is available from the British Library.

This paper meets the requirements of ANSI/NISO Z39.48–1992 (Permanence of Paper).

10   9   8   7   6   5   4   3   2   1

Contents

Introduction

The writers in this volume have one thing in common: all of them were arrested for political crimes in the Soviet Union, and all of them spent years—sometimes many years—in the concentration camp system now known as the Gulag. There, however, their similarities end.

Certainly their backgrounds were very different. Some of them, such as the literary historian Dmitry Likhachev and the ethnographer Nina Gagen-Torn, held prominent positions among the Saint Petersburg intelligentsia. Others, among them Lev Razgon, were ambitious young members of the Bolshevik elite. Still others, including Hava Volovich and Elena Glinka, came from ordinary provincial families. Gustav Herling was a professional writer before his arrest, Isaak Filshtinsky a historian and scholar, Anatoly Zhigulin a poet. Kazimierz Zarod, by contrast, was a civil servant whose only book was his camp memoir.

Inside the camps, too, their experiences were very different. They held a variety of camp jobs, working in forests, mines, factories, and administrative positions. One had a baby; another was the victim of a mass rape. One was a "norm-setter," a person who decided what labor norms other prisoners would have to fulfill. Another spent time in a *sharashka,* a special prison for scientists with a laboratory attached. They played different roles in the hierarchy and the culture of the camps, had different relationships with the professional criminals and the jailers and guards who watched over them. Some were shored up by their faith in God, others by close friendships. Still others kept sane by writing poetry or singing popular songs.

The wide variety of people and voices found in this book is not accidental, for the Gulag itself was an extraordinarily varied place. The word *Gulag* is an acronym: literally, it means "Main Camp Administration." Over time, however, *Gulag* has also come to mean not just the camp administration but the entire Soviet slave-labor complex: labor camps, punishment camps, criminal and political camps, women's camps, children's camps, transit camps, exile villages, Moscow prisons, rural prisons, railway cars. Each of the authors in this book survived at least one of these penal institutions. Some of them survived several.

Most of these essays were written by people who were imprisoned in the Gulag during Stalin's reign, for those were the years when the camp population was the largest, the Gulag's political role the most significant, and its contribution to the Soviet economy the greatest. Indeed, between 1929, when the labor camps first became a mass phenomenon, and 1953, the year of Stalin's death, some 18 million people passed through them. In addition, a further 6 or 7 million were deported to exile villages. In total, the number of people who had some experience of imprisonment in Stalin's Soviet Union could have run as high as 25 million, about 15 percent of the population.[1]

But there had also been earlier camps, set up by Lenin and Feliks Dzerzhinsky in the 1920s as an ad hoc emergency measure to contain "enemies of the people": Dmitry Likhachev survived one of these. And there were later camps, in existence from the time of Stalin's death until the collapse of the Soviet Union in 1991. Some of these, such as the one in which Anatoly Marchenko was imprisoned, became notorious for treating political prisoners with even greater cruelty than had the camps of the earlier era.

The camps had an extraordinary geographical distribution as well. The Gulag's most famous camps were in Siberia and the far North, where prisoners worked in mines and cut timber. But the Gulag also ran camps in central Moscow, where inmates built apartment blocks or designed airplanes; camps in Krasnoyarsk where prisoners ran nuclear power plants; and fishing camps on the Pacific coast. The Gulag photograph albums in the Russian State Archive contain pictures of prisoners with camels, prisoners in the desert, prisoners hoeing vegetables or shucking corn. From Aktyubinsk to Yakutsk, there is hardly a single major population center in the former Soviet Union that did not have its own local camp or camps, or a single industry that did not employ prisoners. Hence the central purpose of this anthology: to provide a sampling of the wide range of life in the Gulag, from transport ships to informers, from pregnancy to forestry.

One word of caution is necessary: some important aspects of the Gulag experience are not reflected in any of these essays. By definition, all the writers featured here survived, and all of them emerged both physically and mentally intact. They were all literate. They were all educated. They all had enough psychological distance from their experience to be able to describe it on paper. Those factors alone make them exceptional. The reader will not find here the testimony of those who died in the camps; those who survived through stealth, murder, or collaboration and could not bear to talk about it afterward; those who were driven mad or physically broken. Although the majority of the Gulag's prisoners, particularly in the early days, were peasants and uneducated workers, their experiences do not feature here either, for the simple reason that they could not write. Nor are there any memoirs of professional criminals: with one or two exceptions, they could not or did not choose to write either. In that sense, this anthology, like other Gulag anthologies, is necessarily skewed, despite the wide range of experiences it encompasses.

All the writers featured here also had a particular motive for putting their experiences down on paper, and that too makes them in some way exceptional. Many of the essays were written soon after the authors returned home, though not necessarily intended for publication. Some did eventually appear in *samizdat*, the underground press, or in foreign editions. But for several decades, these essays could not appear legally in their native countries. Until the 1980s, the only authentic piece of Gulag literature ever published by an official Soviet publishing house was Aleksandr Solzhenitsyn's short novel *A Day in the Life of Ivan Denisovich*. Published in 1962 at the beginning of Nikita Khrushchev's post-Stalinist "Thaw," *Ivan Denisovich* had an unusual career. Originally hailed as a masterpiece and read avidly by former prisoners, it fell under a shadow in 1964 after Leonid Brezhnev ousted Khrushchev as general secretary of the Communist Party and effectively took charge of the Soviet Union. The book was banned along with all other forms of Gulag literature. Throughout the 1970s and 1980s, it was available to Russians only through illegal photocopies, or abroad.

None of Solzhenitsyn's later works—including his *Gulag Archipelago,* a vast, sprawling, oral history of the camps—appeared legally in print either until the final months of the Soviet Union. Official attitudes began to change only in the late 1980s, when the new general secretary, Mikhail Gorbachev, became convinced that his country's problems could be solved only through open discussion. Intending to find solutions to the serious economic, ecological, and social crises the Soviet Union faced, he began encouraging journalists, politicians, and ordinary people to talk and write freely, without censorship. But although Gorbachev's real interest was economic reform, his policy of glasnost, openness, rapidly and perhaps inevitably led to a new discussion of Soviet history. It also led to the publication of dozens, perhaps hundreds, of Gulag memoirs. Most of the works in this book were officially published in Russia for the first time during this period.

These, then, were books written both as literature and as testimony: the authors wanted future generations to know what had happened, even if their writings could not be published in their own lifetime. "As an eyewitness to this century," wrote Likhachev, "it is my human duty to establish the truth about it." Knowing that there would be no official, public acknowledgement of what had happened in the Gulag, they wanted to set the record straight for their children and grandchildren.

In some cases, memoirists also wanted to transmit their experiences in light of a particular personal narrative. Russian prisoners, for example, often experienced their arrests and camp life as a kind of revelation: the cruelties of arrest and the unfairness of incarceration helped them understand the evil of Soviet communism. Both Solzhenitsyn and Yevgenia Ginzburg's renowned memoirs echo this theme. By contrast, foreign prisoners often experienced their arrests as a confirmation of the power of Russian imperialism, and their writing may have had a patriotic impulse as well as a purely historical inspiration.

Memoirists were often people with an acute sense of fairness and justice as well. It is no accident that several of these writers were later involved in the Russian human rights movement, nor is it coincidental that several of them knew Solzhenitsyn, who sought out memoirists in the 1970s when he was working on *The Gulag Archipelago,* at a time when it was dangerous to speak about such things.

The presence of a personal bias does not mean that an author's memoir is false or exaggerated. All authors need a psychological motivation to write, after all. But it does mean that the reader should be aware that the memoirists sometimes had a moral or didactic intent as well as a purely historical purpose. Indeed, some scholars of the Soviet Union have been reluctant to rely on Gulag memoir material as a source of information about the history of the camps, arguing that Soviet memoir writers had political reasons for twisting their stories, that most did their writing many years after their release, and that many borrowed stories from one another when their own memories failed them. Nevertheless, after reading several hundred camp memoirs, and interviewing some two dozen survivors, I do believe that it is possible to filter out those which seem implausible or plagiarized or politicized and that the accounts in this book are essentially truthful.

I also believe that although memoirs cannot be relied on for names, dates, and statistics, they are an invaluable source of other kinds of information. The subtler aspects of camp life—the relationships that prisoners had with one another, with the Gulag administration, and with people on the outside—can be clearly understood only through such accounts. Insights into the psychology of prisoners and the psychology of their guards can be found in these kinds of works and nowhere else. The strange morality of the Gulag—for, as the reader will see, the Gulag did have moral codes of a kind—can also be illustrated only through memoirs. I am aware of no archival document that expresses the emotions of prisoners as well as Gustav Herling's essay on the "houses of meetings," where prisoners were occasionally allowed to spend time with their spouses and families, for example, or Hava Volovich's description of rearing a child born in a camp.

Indeed, I would argue that, far from fading, the significance of Gulag literature grows stronger with time. Many Soviet archives are accessible now, but they tell only the dry, official version of events. Living memories of the society which created the Gulag are beginning to disappear, along with the generation of people who still remember Stalin's Soviet Union. But the best Gulag memoirs continue to provide insights into human nature which are as fresh and relevant as on the day they were written. I hope they will enlighten a new generation.

Other than the first and penultimate essays, the selections in this book do not appear in chronological order: they are designed rather to follow, roughly, the track of a prisoner's experience, from arrest to release, and to illustrate various facets of camp life. Each selection is preceded by a brief description of the author, an explanation of how the memoir came to be written and published, and historical background on the subject. With one or two exceptions all the readings are excerpts of longer works. Footnotes identify key figures, aspects of Gulag history, and camp slang.

There are three notable absences in this book: Solzhenitsyn, Ginzburg, and Varlam Shalamov. Solzhenitsyn is probably the best-known chronicler of the Gulag, but Ginzburg (*Into the Whirlwind*) and Shalamov (*Kolyma Tales*) come a close second. I have not included excerpts from their works because their books are readily available in English. By contrast, the authors in this book are less well known in English, even though some of their works have been translated and a few have been best-selling authors in Poland (Herling) or Russia (Razgon, Zhigulin, Likhachev).

Yet even these better-known writers have lately been eclipsed by other subjects, other issues, and their work can be hard to find even in their own countries. The Gulag is not a fashionable topic in contemporary Russia, and the vast body of Gulag literature is for the most part not read in Russian schools or universities. Though this book is intended for an English-speaking audience, it is also my hope that by reprinting and recognizing these writers, I can help their names endure longer in the country where they spent so many years behind barbed wire.

NOTES

1. See Anne Applebaum, *Gulag: A History* (New York: Anchor, 2004), 578–86, for further statistics about labor camp populations.

Gulag Voices

I.

DMITRY S. LIKHACHEV

To describe Dmitry Likhachev as a former Gulag prisoner is a little bit like describing Albert Einstein as a talented amateur violinist: he was that, but also so much more. Likhachev was born in 1906 and belonged to the extraordinarily cultured world of prerevolutionary Saint Petersburg. Like many of his contemporaries, he was arrested in 1928 for taking part in an academic discussion circle and was thus one of the early victims of the Bolsheviks' systematic destruction of Russian civil society. In the view of the Soviet secret police, any organized group, even one devoted to the discussion of literature—Likhachev's fellow club members saluted one another in ancient Greek— was by definition an enemy of the state. Accordingly, they accused Likhachev of planning counter-revolutionary activity. He served out his sentence on the Solovetsky Islands, the Soviet Union's first political prison.

In one sense Likhachev was lucky: he survived his experience and did not fall victim to the waves of mass execution that washed over Solovetsky from time to time. He was released in 1932. In the years that followed, he slowly rose to public prominence, becoming Russia's best-known literary historian, critic, and scholar. He wrote hundreds of books and articles, touching on everything from medieval icons to the architecture of Saint Petersburg. By the time of his death, in 1999, he had become a national institution.

His description of the four years he spent in the Solovetsky camps also constitutes a significant contribution to Russian culture because of what it reveals about the earliest days of the Gulag. The Solovetsky camps, known by the acronym SLON (Solovetsky Camp of Special Significance), were located on an archipelago in the White Sea and were the first prisons to be entirely controlled by the Soviet secret police. Here a notorious group of policemen also began experimenting with the forced-labor system. Prisoners in the camps cultivated furs for export, cut trees, and canned fish. They were "paid" for their labor with rations: those who worked harder received more food, those who could not work received less and eventually starved to death. The commercial success of Solovetsky and the rationing first put into use there helped persuade Stalin to expand the entire camp system in 1929. Using Solovetsky as a model, he aimed to use slave labor to mine Russia's natural resources, to boost the Soviet economy, and to terrorize the population as well.

As Likhachev's writing make clear, these early camps had an experimental feel. Rules were unpredictable, guards were irrational, prisoners might be treated well or badly, and it was hard to say why. Although some prisoners were able to publish magazines and conduct scientific experiments—at one point the main island contained a botanical garden as well as a mink farm—prisoners unable to fulfill their work assignments died of starvation. Murder and torture were common.

Likhachev wrote several essays about his years on the islands, including a famous linguistic investigation of the slang used by the criminals incarcerated alongside him. These essays were all published in the late 1980s, after Gorbachev came to power. The essay reprinted here describes Likhachev's arrest in February 1928 and illustrates the odd, slovenly atmosphere of the pre-Stalinist Soviet prison system.

Arrest

It was early February 1928. The clock in our flat on Oraniyenbaumskaya Street struck eight. I was alone at home, and was suddenly seized by an icy dread. I had not the least idea why. I had just heard the sound of the clock for the very first time. My father didn't like to hear the clock strike, and the chimes had been turned off even before I was born. Why had the clock decided to strike for me for the first time in twenty-one years with its measured solemnity?

They came for me on the eighth of February early in the morning; there was a uniformed investigator and Sabelnikov, commandant of our buildings at the Pechatny

Dvor.[1] The latter was terribly upset (the same fate befell him later), but the investigator was polite and even sympathetic toward my parents, especially when my father turned pale and collapsed into the leather armchair in his study. The investigator took him a glass of water, and it was a long time before I could shake off my feelings of acute pity for my father.

The search itself didn't take long. The investigator checked a piece of paper that he had, confidently approached the bookshelf, and pulled down H. Ford's *International Jewry*[2] in its red binding. It all became clear to me: one of my university acquaintances had called for no particular reason a week before my arrest, looked at my books, and asked, with a voluptuous smile, whether I had anything anti-Soviet. He assured me that he was terribly keen on such lack of taste and vulgarity.

My mother put some things together (soap, underwear, warm clothes), and we bid each other good-bye. As everyone does in these situations I said, "This is madness, it'll soon be sorted out, and I'll be back soon." But at the time mass and irreversible arrests were in full swing.

In the black Ford, then quite a novelty in Leningrad, we drove past the Exchange. By that time it was getting light,

1. A printing house founded by Tsar Nicholas I, still in operation after the Revolution.

2. A reference to Henry Ford's *The International Jew*, one of a series of virulently antisemitic books written by the founder of the American automobile industry. It describes Jews as both vicious capitalists and vicious Bolsheviks.

and the deserted city was unusually lovely. The investigator said nothing. Anyway, why am I calling him that? My real investigator was Aleksandr (Albert) Robertovich Stromin, who was behind all the prosecutions of the intelligentsia of the late 1920s, served in Saratov as head of the NKVD,[3] and was shot "as a Trotskyist" in 1938.

After being searched and relieved of my cross, my silver watch, and a few rubles, I was taken to a cell on the fifth floor of the DPZ building[4] in Shpalernaya Street (on the outside this building has three floors, but for the purpose of preventing escapes the building stands in a sort of tank). The cell was no. 273—the same as absolute zero.

At university I had been a friend of Lev Karsavin,[5] and when I got to the DPZ I found myself, as fate would have it, in the same cell as the brother of a woman friend of his. I remember that boy: he wore a velvet jacket and sang Gypsy ballads in a fine voice, quietly, so that the warders shouldn't hear. Shortly before I had been reading Karsavin's book *Noctes Petropolitanae*.

The good six months I spent in that cell was the hardest period of my life. It was hard psychologically. But it was a time when I met a huge number of people who lived by quite different principles.

3. Commissariat of Internal Affairs, the acronym for the domestic Soviet secret police, earlier referred to as Cheka or OGPU and later variously known as the MGB, from Ministry of State Security, and the KGB.

4. The investigative prison in Leningrad.

5. Lev Karsavin (1882–1952) was a Russian religious philosopher and medieval historian.

I will mention a few of my cellmates. In cell 273, in-tended for one occupant, and into which I was thrown, there was an energetic *nepman*[6] by the name of Kotliar, a shop owner of some description. He'd been arrested the previous day (this was the period when NEP was being abolished). He immediately proposed that we clean up the cell. The air there was dreadfully foul, and the walls, which had once been painted, were black with fungus. The lavatory seat was filthy and had not been cleaned for a long time. Kotliar asked the warders for some rags, and a day or two later they threw us somebody's woolen underpants. Kotliar suggested that they'd been stripped off someone who had been shot. Choking back the nausea in our throats we set about scrap-ing the mildew off the walls and washing the floor, which was soft with filth, but the main objective was cleaning the lavatory. Two days' hard labor did the trick, and the result was a cell filled with fresh air. The third person to be pushed into our "one-man" cell was a professional thief. When I was summoned at night for interrogation he advised me to put my coat on (I had with me my father's warm winter coat lined with squirrel fur). "At interrogations you've got to keep warm—you'll feel calmer." The interrogation was my only one (if you don't count the filling up of questionnaires beforehand). I sat there in my coat as if in armor. Stromin,

---

6. In 1921 Lenin launched his New Economic Policy (NEP), which re-stored a limited amount of free enterprise and private business to the Soviet Union, but the policy was ended by Stalin. "Nepmen," always suspicious fig-ures, were small-time entrepreneurs who tried to take advantage of the policy.

the investigator (the organizer, as I've already said, of all the actions of the late '20s and early '30s against the intelligentsia, including the unsuccessful "academic" one), failed to extract from me any of the information that he wanted (my parents were told, "Your son's behaving badly"). At the start of the interrogation he asked me, "Why are you wearing your coat?" I replied, "I've got a cold" (that was what the thief had told me to say). Stromin was evidently afraid of catching influenza, as it was then called, and the interrogation didn't last long enough to be exhausting.

Later we had a Chinese boy in the cell (for some reason there were a lot of Chinese in DPZ in 1928), from whom I tried unsuccessfully to learn Chinese; Count Rochefort (such seems to have been his surname), a descendant of the man who set up the tsarist prison system; a peasant boy who'd come to town for the first time and had taken a "suspicious" interest in a seaplane, the like of which he'd never before seen. And numerous others. Interest in all these people kept me going.

For six months our cell was taken for exercise by "Granddad," as we called him, who had done the same for many revolutionaries under the tsarist government. Once he got to know us he showed us the cells where various famous revolutionaries had been held. I regret that I made no attempt at remembering the numbers. "Granddad" was a stern veteran, but he took part in the warders' favorite game—passing a live rat back- and forward among themselves with brooms. When a warder noticed a rat running across the yard he would start to sweep it with a broom until it died of exhaustion. If there were other warders present they would join in the hunt and pass the rat from one to another, shouting as they did so, sweeping it toward an imaginary goal. This sadistic sport roused the warders to a rare pitch of excitement. The rat would immediately try to get away, escape, but they would keep on sweeping it, screaming and yelling all the time. The prisoners could watch this through the "muzzles" in the cells and compare the fate of the rat with their own.

After six months the investigation was over, and I was transferred to the general library cell. There were many extremely interesting people there, including N. P. Antsiferov,[7] although, as he points out in his memoirs, I had already left by the time he arrived. We slept on the floor, even right by the lavatory pedestal, and for amusement we took turns to present "papers" with following discussion. The habit of discussing questions of general interest, which members of the Russian intelligentsia never tired of, sustained them even in the prisons and the camps. The papers were all on every kind of extravagant subject, and their theses were in sharp contradiction to accepted views. This was a characteristic feature of all papers delivered in prison and camp. The most impossible theories were dreamed up. I too delivered a paper, my theme being that every man determines his own fate even when events seemed to occur at random. Thus it was that all the Romantic poets died young—Keats,

---

7. N. P. Antsiferov (1889–1958) was a Russian historian and ethnographer.

Shelley, Lermontov,[8] etc. They had, as it were, thrust themselves upon death and misfortune. Lermontov had even begun to limp on the same leg as Byron. I also expressed my views on the comparative longevity of Zhukovsky. Realists, by contrast, lived long. And we, following the traditions of the Russian intelligentsia, had brought about our own arrests. It was our "free-will fate." . . .

The most interesting man in the library cell was the head of the Petrograd Boy Scouts, Count Vladimir Mikhailovich Shuvalov. I had met him now and then in the streets just after the Revolution in Scout uniform, with his long Scout pole and distinctive hat. Now, in the cell, he was gloomy but strong and smart. He was studying logic. As far as I recall these were notions continuing Husserl's *Researches in Logic*. I don't understand how he was able to shut himself off from the dreadful noise in his cell and concentrate on his studies. He must have had great willpower and enthusiasm. When he expounded the results of his thinking I had difficulty in understanding him, although I had studied logic under Vvedensky and, like Shuvalov himself, Povarin.[9]

Eventually he was exiled, and I never saw him again. I think that a relative of his, or perhaps his wife, worked on the icons in the Russian Museum.

8. Mikhail Lermontov (1814–41) was a prominent late-Romantic poet and painter; Vasily Zhukovsky (below; 1783–1852) the preeminent early-Romantic poet.

9. Aleksandr Vvedensky (1904–41) was a Russian avant-garde poet and philosopher; S. I. Povarin was a prerevolutionary logician.

When you consider, our jailers did some strange things. Having arrested us for meeting at the most once a week to spend a few hours in discussion of philosophical, artistic, and religious questions that aroused our interest, first of all they put us all together in a prison cell and then in camps and swelled our numbers with others from our city interested in the resolution of the same philosophical questions, while in the camps we were mixed with a wide and generous range of such people from Moscow, Rostov, the Caucasus, the Crimea, and Siberia. We passed through a gigantic school of mutual education before vanishing once more in the limitless expanses of our Motherland.

In the library cell, where people were sent on completion of investigation to await sentence, I saw Nonconformists, Baptists (one of these had crossed the frontier from somewhere in the West, was expecting to be shot and couldn't sleep at night), Satanists (there really were such people), Theosophists, homespun Masons (they used to meet somewhere on the Bolshoi Prospekt in the Petrograd District and prayed to the sound of the cello; how vulgar, if I might say so!). The OGPU satirists, the "Tur brothers," tried now and then to show us in a ridiculous and insulting light; they published a piece about us in *Leningradskaia Pravda*, thick with lies, entitled "Oaken Ashes" and one entitled "The Light Blue International" about some of the others, and so on. M. M. Bakhtin later wrote in his memoirs about "Oaken Ashes."

Our relatives too gathered, meeting at transfer points and at various little windows where information about us was given out, or more often was not. They were advised what to hand over, what to give us for when we stopped, where and what to provide for their prisoners. Many made friends. By that time we could guess how much they were going to give and to whom.

One day we were all summoned "without belongings" to the governor of the prison. In a deliberately lugubrious tone, specially assumed for the occasion, he read out our sentences. We stood and listened. Igor Yevgenevich Anichkov was absolutely priceless. With a markedly uninterested air he looked at the paper on the office wall, the ceiling, anywhere but at the governor, and when the latter had finished reading and was expecting us to hurl ourselves upon him with the usual lamentations—"We're innocent," "We shall demand a proper trial and a proper defense," and the like—Anichkov, who had received five years like myself, asked with exaggerated indifference, "Is that all? May we go?" and, without waiting for a reply, turned and walked toward the door, taking us with him to the complete bewilderment of the governor and the escorts, who took a while to recover. It was magnificent!

About a fortnight after sentences had been pronounced we were all summoned "with belongings" (on Solovky the call was different: "Fly out like a bullet with your things") and sent off in Black Marias[10] to the Nikolayevsky (now Moskovsky) Station. We drew up at the extreme right platform,

10. Trucks used for transporting prisoners.

from which the dacha trains now leave. One at a time we got out of the Black Marias and a crowd that was there to see us off in the twilight (it was an October evening) shouted, as they recognized each of us, "Kolya!" "Dima!" "Volodya!" Soldiers who formed the escort, bayonets fixed, drove back the crowd of parents, friends, and colleagues from school or work. Two soldiers, brandishing their bayonets, walked up and down in front of the crowd while one escort passed us over to the other, checking off the list. They put us in two Stolypin cars,[11] which had been considered terrible in tsarist times but in the Soviet era had gained a reputation for actually being comfortable. When we had finally been crammed into our cages another escort began handing out everything that our relations had brought us. I got a big confectioners' cake from the university library, and some flowers too. When the train moved from behind the bars the head of the commander of the escort appeared (Oh bliss!) and said in a friendly manner, "Look here, lads, don't hold it against us: it's orders. What if we don't get the counting done?" Somebody answered, "All right, but why start on the people seeing us off with swearing and bayonets?"

11. Cars used for transporting prisoners. Also called "Stolypinki," they were named for Pyotr Stolypin (1862–1911), prime minister of tsarist Russia 1906–11.

2.

ALEXANDER DOLGUN

Alexander Dolgun's story will shock many modern American readers, not least because of what it reveals about the past practices of their own government. Dolgun was an American, born in the Bronx in 1926. In 1933, in the depths of the Depression, his unemployed father, Michael Dolgun, moved to the Soviet Union to take a job as a technician at the Moscow Automotive Works. After a year he brought over his American wife and children. It was a disastrous decision: when they tried to return home, Soviet bureaucrats prevented the family from leaving the country. Both Michael and his wife spent the rest of their lives in the Soviet Union. Alexander, who went to work as a clerk at the U.S. embassy, was arrested in 1948, "kidnapped," as he put it, right off the street. He remained incarcerated until 1956, but even after his release he was not allowed to leave the country. During that time and the decades that followed, no member of the U.S. government and none of Dolgun's former embassy colleagues made the

slightest attempt to help him. In the days before the birth of
the modern human rights movement and Amnesty International, diplomats rarely concerned themselves with the fate
of private U.S. citizens.

Dolgun did finally return to the United States in 1971,
thanks to the efforts of his sister, who had escaped the Soviet Union by marrying a British diplomat, and aided as
well by the onset of détente. His memoir, *Alexander Dolgun's Story,* caused a small sensation when it was published
in 1975. But although there are many arresting passages—
the perspective of an American in the Soviet Gulag is an
unusual one, to say the least—the most famous part of the
book is Dolgun's description of his interrogation. Dolgun
had been a young embassy employee with a mischievous
streak who "borrowed" cars from the embassy garage and
books from library and would sneak into parties with older
staff. From this the Soviet secret police concluded that he
must be a spy: no low-ranking clerk could otherwise have
the kind of access Dolgun did. As a result, his case was
treated with grim seriousness. Among other things, Dolgun
was interrogated in Sukhanovka, a prison and torture cham-
ber from which few emerged either alive or sane. Other
prisoners considered Dolgun's survival so exceptional that
Solzhenitsyn sought out his testimony when writing *The
Gulag Archipelago.*

The selection that follows describes an earlier period of
Dolgun's interrogation, in Lefortovo Prison. Some elements
of his interrogation were unique; others are recognizable
from descriptions by other prisoners. Usually the goal of

Soviet interrogations was to get prisoners to confess, no matter how improbable the charges or how innocent they might know the prisoner to be. The interrogators' purpose in these cases seems to have been twofold: to gather further evidence—the confession invariably included a condemnation of other members of the conspiracy—and to reassure the interrogators of the validity, moral and legal, of their methods. If a prisoner confessed, after all, then he or she must be guilty.

Dolgun describes the methods he used to resist confessing—and to stay sane. Among other things he sang popular songs, hid his face under a hat to "train" the guards not to recognize when he was snatching an extra hour or two of illicit sleep, and "walked" from his prison cell in Moscow to America, counting tens of thousands of steps. He also made a "calendar" using dried bread balls and matchsticks.

Eventually, he even learned the prisoners' "Morse code," tapped on the walls between cells, and was able to communicate with the prisoner next door to him. Invented in tsarist Russia, this code remained in use throughout the Gulag era, and even afterward (Senator John McCain remembers using the same code in the prisons of North Vietnam). Dolgun learned it the way most prisoners did—from the prisoner in the neighboring cell. In the excerpt reprinted here he begins to work out the code; later he would come to understand that each group of "taps" represented a different letter of the Russian alphabet.

Interrogation

Toward the end of the first month in Lefortovo things began to get very bad. Except on the weekends, I was never able to steal more than at the most an hour of sleep every day, and looking back it seems that an hour is too much; it may have been no more than a few minutes some nights. Effectively it was the same as no sleep at all, and my mind began to go blank fairly frequently. The effort to keep counting my steps and converting them to kilometers and remember where I had stopped walking the day before was almost more than I could summon up. My eyes pained constantly, both burning and aching. Sudden bright light was an agony. In the singing periods, I would find myself drifting off into incoherent mutterings and then I would have to lecture myself very sharply to get back on the road. One day I became acutely terrified sitting on my bunk staring at the wall. The wall had been painted and repainted to try to obliterate the scratches of earlier residents of the psychic cell.[1] The traces of half-obscured scratchings combined with cracks running through the masonry made patterns that my mind naturally reshaped into concrete images, the way the interlaced lines in the patterned wallpaper used to turn into ships and animals and cars when I lay in bed as a child. One pattern had begun to fascinate me. If I stared long enough at a certain section of the wall I would begin to see the face of an old man emerge from the random

1. The isolation cell.

scars and etchings. At first it was agreeable to look for this pattern and relax and wait for the old face to take shape in the half light. Later it began to look like an evil face, but I still looked for it sometimes out of a vague curiosity. What frightened me that day suddenly was that the face, as I stared at it, narrowed its eyes and curled back its lips in a fierce and menacing silent snarl. The hallucination was quite real. The intentions of this evil old creature were clear. He intended to hurt me somehow. But the fear that started my heart beating fast and sent me walking up and down the cell and counting like mad was not the same fear as in a nightmare, when you believe in the terrible things you dream and are in a real way pursued by them. My fear was that I was going out of my mind. I was enormously, morbidly afraid of going crazy.

Sidorov[2] had increased the intensity of his questioning at night. He had begun to suggest that I was particularly interested in certain Soviet naval officers. He told me that my association with a navy lieutenant at our own embassy, Bob Dreyer, a guy I often went out with, drinking and dancing and so on, was suspect because they had long had him marked as an intelligence agent. Not long before I was kidnapped, Dreyer had gotten into trouble over our stores warehouse. The MGB accused him, falsely, of peddling embassy stores on the black market. He was declared persona non grata, and the embassy had been forced to ship him back to the United States.

2. Dolgun's interrogator.

Sidorov would say, "We have indisputable evidence that you were engaged in espionage activities with Bob Dreyer. Why do you deny it?"

My answer: "I deny it, that's all."

All this futile dialogue was dutifully recorded on protocols, day after day, and brought across the room for me to read and sign. Sidorov was angry all the time at night. He was angry at each denial, angry at the changing signature, angry at my silences while I tried desperately to shut out my hunger and my confusion and my searing need for sleep by concentration on my arithmetic and my line across the map of western Russia.

One morning when I stumbled into the cell it was so cold I could see my breath. Now I had to increase the pace of my walking to keep warm, and since I was losing weight on the miserable rations, I had little fuel in my body to burn for warmth.

But even with all these growing threats to my stamina and my mind, I still believed I would find some way to get some sleep and that, once found, it would keep me going in spite of everything they could hit me with.

Sidorov had produced a collection of photographs, mostly of army and navy officers, Soviets, in uniform, and began to show them to me one after another during interrogation, demanding that I identify these unknown men and cursing me when I said I did not recognize any of them.

Over and over again, the same photographs, street photographs taken surreptitiously, formal photographs in a studio, face after face of strangers. Over and over again, with the sense of violence coming nearer and nearer to the surface. "I'm giving you another chance. We know you know some of these men. Point out the ones you know! Those were taken in 1945. Why do you deny that you know some of these men!"

My answer: "I deny it."

Sign the protocol.

Sidorov would tell me, correctly, that I was very knowledgeable about Soviet ships and planes. He would quiz me about this: tonnages, armaments, and so on. I don't know now whether it was foolish to answer him accurately, but I did. If agents in the embassy, and it became clear that in one case a charwoman, as well as many others, had reported on my reading and my conversations, then there was no point claiming I was ignorant in military and especially naval matters. They were a hobby with me, and anyone who had been around the embassy would know about it. Sidorov claimed that the books I had taken from the embassy library—like *Jane's Fighting Ships* and *Jane's All the World's Aircraft* and so on—marked me as a spy for sure, and he would not believe me when I told him that in a free country you could buy such books in any bookstore. I told him that thousands of young kids in the States memorized the details of planes and ships just as others memorized batting averages and other baseball details, but he just accused me of lying to cover up my "demonstrated anti-Soviet activities."

And then, around three in the morning, he put photographs on my little table and yelled at me from across the room to keep turning them over until I was prepared to admit that there was someone in the collection I recognized. I sighed and put my head down and began to turn them over. I said, "It's no use; we've done this over and over. I don't recognize anyone. Not one!" I kept turning the photographs over dumbly, placing them face down after I had scanned them. I did not see him come at me until it was too late to throw up my hands or duck. His fist came in hard and caught me on the side of the face with enough force to spin me right out of my chair and onto the floor. I was dizzy with the shock of the blow. I lay as still as I could on the floor with my hands over my eyes and my head pounding. The blow was still reverberating inside my skull. Sidorov barked, "Liar! Liar! Liar!" He came and stood over me where I huddled in the corner. "Get up!" he screamed. "Get up and go through them again and again until you come to your senses and confess you know him!"

"Who? Who?" I yelled back at him, still on the floor. "I never saw any of these men! None of them!"

Suddenly I felt as if my right shin had been cracked open. I sat up and grabbed for it, almost screaming myself, when the toe of his hard high boot landed on the other shin. I felt sick and my stomach began to heave but there was nothing in it to bring up. I got to my hands and knees somehow. My eyes were blurred and red and I could vaguely see his feet scuffing the floor beside me. I was afraid he was going to kick again. I knew I could never stand another blow on top of the first. I pushed myself up as hard as I could, breathing hard and fast to keep the tears back and to keep from yelling.

"The photographs!" he screamed. And hardly able to see them at all, I bent over them again. I had begun to *believe* that there was someone here I should recognize. I knew, too, that his continual insistence that I knew someone in these pictures could lead me to believe it even if it was not so. I was determined not to be trapped like that. My hands were shaking with anger and pain, but I started going through the photographs as quickly as I could, identifying the few streets or buildings I recognized, and muttering, "I'll try, I'll try as hard as I can." Sidorov paced the room. I bent my head hard over the pictures so he could not see my face. I worked at composing myself. Gradually I got my heartbeat slowed down and my breathing a good deal easier. I really peered closely at those pictures. I waited until Sidorov got tired of walking and sat down, and then I looked right in his eyes and smiled a big smile. I said, "Maybe you've got some better pictures?" His eyes went very narrow. I was taking the risk of another fist or a boot, but I knew that this was the precise moment when I had to show him he was not winning. He did not get up out of his chair. He did not yell. He just stared. I think there might have been a faint hint of admiration in that stare.

Back in the frigid cell I rolled up my pants and looked at my shins. The left was angry red and bruised. The right was cut open, and when I pulled up the long prison underwear, a bit of clotted blood was pulled off and a thin trickle

of blood began to ooze. I washed it in cold water. It seemed a little before six. My head was pounding terribly. I was shivering and nauseated. I climbed under the blanket and *willed* that there should be time for sleep. For a while my pounding head kept me awake with a sensation of lights pulsing. Then I dropped off and slept for perhaps ten or twenty minutes before the slot opened and that squat, ugly hag[3] yelled at me.

The moment I opened my eyes the pain began again. The hag brought my coat for exercise time, and I said I wanted to stay in the cell, that I felt sick.

"*Ne polozheno!*"[4]

I went out and shut my eyes against the hard light in the corridors to cut down the pain. Somehow I remembered to count. I was in the countryside, dodging towns big enough to have a police station, and beginning to wonder what it would be like when I had to negotiate the border. But that was a long way off. I had only made about forty or fifty kilometers [twenty-five to thirty miles], but it was a relief to have Moscow far behind me.

Breakfast made me more nauseated, but I worked at keeping it down. I feverishly worked a few minutes on my calendar. I prayed for the wind tunnel[5] to start up so I could shout out some curses, tell some jokes, sing a rousing song.

3. One of the guards.
4. "Forbidden!"
5. The "wind tunnel" was Dolgun's term for a noise he heard periodically, possibly caused by some kind of heater or fan.

At the same time I was afraid the noise might split my head. The wind tunnel did not start. No wing-stress research today, I told myself.

I drank the hot colored water with the sugar in it and I drank a lot of cold water and urinated a lot. I felt my shins. They were exquisitely tender. When I washed and ran my fingers through my hair some more hair came out, a little tuft. Now, running my fingers over my scalp, I thought I could feel three tiny bald spots. That seemed a sign of serious physical deterioration and made my heart beat pretty fast, so I forced myself to sit on the bunk and stare at the peephole and lecture myself silently on calming down. I took long, measured breaths. Somehow, by a quarter to ten, when I signed in at the iron book,[6] the pain in my head had gone down a good deal, but when I closed my eyes I could still see lights pulsing.

Sidorov came in late. He said "Good morning," as if nothing had happened. "Are you ready to confess everything now?"

"I have nothing to confess." I forced a smile at that hated face. "You may as well realize that I have nothing to confess and I never will. Then we could talk about something else or you could let me get some sleep!"

"We'll see."

A totally inconsequential day. Sidorov yawned a lot. That was hard on me. I yawned all the time and rubbed my

---

6. A register that Dolgun had to sign before every interrogation.

eyes over and over. Almost routinely I fell on the floor, in a dead sleep. Sometimes I think Sidorov left me there long enough to get deep into my sleep before he called a guard to pour cold water on my neck. The shock of the water made my heart beat so hard I thought that I could hear it.

We got through the day. I was helped back to the cell because I stumbled so much. My vision was quite blurred. Strangely, I wanted to read. Words, for human contact. I looked for my books. They were gone. I knocked on the cell door. The woman had gone off duty and a reasonably decent guy opened the slot. "My books!" I mumbled in a piteous kind of voice. He must have thought I was crazy. He just shook his head and closed the slot. The books were never returned, and I never got another issue.

When I ate the cold soup, I immediately vomited. I drank some water and then carefully tried a few mouthfuls of bread saved from the morning. They stayed down. When porridge came I ate it with the greatest care, slowly. It stayed down.

I wanted to continue walking to America but I was too weak. I washed my face several times. I willed myself to sleep sitting up straight and probably caught a few minutes, but then I heard the slot open and the guard said firmly, "Ne polozheno." Somehow I thought that was funny so I laughed a weak laugh at him and said, "I know, I know," and waved him away. I fumbled with my calendar and tried to remember whether I had changed the date that morning. I remembered that I had not made the scratch for the day on the cumulative record, so I did that. Then I tried to add the days up and determine what day this was, to make sure the numbers were right on the bread calendar. But I kept forgetting the totals and gave it up.

Rubbing my head, I got another idea. It came out of nowhere. I felt the bare patches and looked at the hairs on my fingers and suddenly got some energy from a discovery that might save my mind. I knocked on the door again, and the moderately easygoing guard came back and looked in. I steadied my voice as well as I could and told him that I had a serious scalp condition and that if I did not see a doctor soon it could become really bad. I bent over and let him look at my patchwork scalp. He did not answer, but he went away and came back with the block supervisor, who also looked at my scalp. I could hear them confer outside. I remember being cheered, as I always was by the arrival of a new idea for surviving, all the way back to the interrogation room at ten o'clock that night. But the cheer did not last ten seconds inside the room.

Sidorov did not even wait for a denial. He waded into me with both fists, yelling at me that if I did not tell him everything he would kill me with his bare hands.

He sent me flailing across the room trying to hold my balance, which was not very good to begin with. I hit the wall hard and went down on my knees. I thought, I must protect my shins! I must protect my shins! Sidorov picked me up by the shoulders and dragged me to my chair, screaming obscenities. He dumped me in the chair and slapped my cheeks hard, yelling at me to sit up straight. I held my eyes closed against the shattering pain of the lights in the room. He slapped me again and yelled at me to open my eyes.

I tried to force a smile, but my lips felt numb where his fist had caught me. I wiped my mouth, and there was a trail of blood on the back of my hand. Sidorov stood over me with his face close to mine.

"Are you going to identify the man?" he said, with a sudden quiet in his voice.

I did not trust my voice. I just shook my head and mouthed the words, "I can't."

The shock when his boot hit my shin on top of the first bruise made me gasp. The next kick made me yell out loud. "Please! Please! How can I tell you names I don't know! Please! I'll tell you any name! Boris, Andrei, I don't know. Anything, only please don't kick again!"

The fist lashed out again and my consciousness just swam away. I have a vague memory of someone fumbling with a stethoscope at my chest, and fingers peeling back my burning eyelids. Then I know I was dragged down the hall and across to the cell block by two guards holding me under the arms. I would come to and pass out as they dragged me up the stairs. They dumped me on the floor of my cell. I smelled vomit and then realized it was on the front of my shirt. I felt parched and nauseated at the same time. I managed to get to my knees, although the blinding blows inside my skull had sent my balance all off and the movement made me dizzy. I turned on the tap and let some water run down my cheeks and swallowed a little of it. My stomach heaved and it came back up.

My soaked shirt chilled my upper body. I began to shiver terribly. The asphalt floor was terribly cold, but every time I tried to crawl to the bed I felt dizzy and sick.

For a long time I lay shivering on that floor. Then a strange thing happened. The pain receded. I was perfectly conscious. I was standing in the corner of the cell looking down at a shivering, vomit-covered wreck in the corner by the reeking toilet. There was blood on his face and his lip was swollen. There were bare pink patches on his scalp. He moaned with every breath, and from time to time his body arched and his stomach heaved a dry heave. And I thought, "That poor son of a bitch! Look how he suffers! But he doesn't cry. He won't give them *that* satisfaction."

I quite clearly stood outside myself and my suffering. It is my clearest recollection of that pulsing and blinding and confused and agony-filled night. For a while I had clarity and peace. I watched my own body suffer. And when the suffering subsided a little and the moans stopped and the eyes opened and seemed to focus, I got back in the body and dragged myself to the bed and climbed in and blessed the warmth of the blanket, and left my hands outside, and slept without moving.

When "*Podyom*"[7] was shouted, I went to sit up, but my head was pounding again and I had to go very slowly. When they saw that I could scarcely walk, they let the exercise period go by. I found I could eat my bread, through a mixture of burning hunger and twinges of nausea. The hot tea seemed to help my head. I wanted to look at my shins. One had red and purple bruises. The other was cemented to my underpants with blood, and I left it alone.

---

7. "Wake up!"

When the wind tunnel began to wind up, it startled me, and I was afraid that the noise would hurt my head. When it hit full volume, I felt a sudden sense of release and I had a terrible urge to cry, but I was damned if they would see me cry. I thought, Quick! What's the most rousing song I know? And then I limped up and down the cell, feeling stronger as I worked some of the stiffness out of my lower legs, and I sang,

Roll! Out! The barr-elll!
We'll have a barrel of fun!

I roared:

Roll out the barrel!
We've got the blues on the run.

A great song! A song I came to trust. I could feel the need for tears pushing hard from somewhere inside, but I pushed back with the song.

Zing! Boom! Tararrel!
We'll have a barrel of cheer!

Stomping up the cell like a drum major, I brought my hand up and down with an invisible baton. To hell with them if they were watching. Let them watch. I stared hard at the peephole until it opened and forced a huge smile on my face as the astonished eyes peered.

Now's the time to roll the barrel
Because the gang's! All! He-e-e-ere!

I fully expected the guard to come in. He didn't. That was the first time I realized that the chief reason for the prohibition against talking and singing must be to keep other prisoners from hearing me. From then on I sang openly toward the peephole as long as the wind tunnel was roaring.

Suddenly the door opened and a doctor came in. "What's all this about your hair?" he shouted over the wind tunnel. I shouted back. He motioned a guard and they took me out on the catwalk, where the light was better, and shut the door against the noise.

I explained as convincingly as I could that this was an old ailment that ran in my family and was brought on by cold. I made up a story. I said that I did not know if it was true, but that two of my cousins were said to have died of brain inflammations after all their hair had fallen out and that was why the whole family always wore hats all the time in cold weather. I said I had been wearing a hat when I was arrested but that it had been taken away. I must have been very convincing. Perhaps my shattered-looking state helped. In any case, the miracle took place. When I came back to the cell in the late afternoon (after a completely routine day with Sidorov, in which he announced that for the time being he would change the line of interrogation and that for the next several sessions we would discuss my work as a file clerk and the nature of the information I had access to), my hat was on my bunk! My beautiful, wide-brimmed, American-made fedora! I savored the word. *Fedora!* The hat was a bit crushed from being bundled up, but the brim snapped out, and I soon had it worked into something like its original shape. I parked it jauntily on my aching head and sat on the bunk facing the door. The brim eclipsed the little bulb over the door, and I knew that my eyes were in shadow. The light was so weak I was sure that my eyes would be invisible to the guard at the peephole. When the peephole opened, I sat absolutely immobile. The guard seemed to wait a bit longer than usual, but then closed it and moved off. I thought, he's waiting to see if I've moved when he comes back. I did not move. He was back in a minute. I concentrated hard and sat motionless, trying to guess how long he would watch before he assumed I was trying to sleep. Just before I thought he was going to open the slot and yell, after he watched me for twice as long as usual, I raised my hand and wiped the back of it across my nose. The peephole closed. I spent the rest of the evening before going to Sidorov conditioning the guard that way. Every time he looked in he watched a little longer than usual, and every time I gave a sign of movement at the last moment. I was terribly tempted just to go off to sleep, now that I was confident I could do it without falling over, but I talked myself out of it. *Easy, kid. You had several hours under the blanket last night, even if you were beaten up. Don't rush it. One false move and they'll take that hat. This is going to save your life if it works. So you can go a little longer, just a little longer, keep it up, a few more days, that's all.*

I began to feel a hard knot in my stomach as the time came closer to go back to interrogation. I gingerly felt my shins and I knew I would scream if Sidorov kicked me again, as I fully expected he would. I did not know how I could possibly stand more of that, but maybe I would pass out again. Or maybe with a new topic I would be able to tell him things he wanted to know without compromising myself, and put off the beatings for a while. As it turned out, the next two nights were not so bad. He tried to get me to admit that as chief file clerk of the consular section I had access to coded information, and I kept insisting that the code room was separate, which he no doubt knew, and that I never saw anything classified, which was not true.

First thing in the morning I put on the hat and went on with the process of conditioning the guards. The nice young Komsomol[8] was on, and he just left me alone. He probably knew what I was up to, I don't know. But he never even lingered at the peephole, and I took the chance and got an hour's sleep sitting up. My back ached when I forced myself awake, but my head felt a little clearer. Then came a hell of a day with the woman, who, I understood, would never be conditioned, and then it was Saturday night again.

Sidorov, as he often did, stopped the interrogation early on Saturday, and when I got back to the cell, even though the ugly squat one harassed me for the rest of her duty period, I had the consolation of the wind tunnel, which ran full blast

---

8. The Komsomol was the Communist youth organization.

that day until after six in the afternoon. I had another inspiration. I imagined Sidorov striding off down the street outside Lefortovo to his wife or his mistress, and I saluted his retreating back in my mind and shouted out loud, "Sidorov, you bastard, this song is dedicated to you!"

Then I sang all I could remember of

Saturday night is the loneliest night of the week,
'Cause that's the night that my baby and I
Used to dance cheek to cheek.

I sang it ironically, not in the spirit of the original. It was my celebration of Sidorov's departure for the weekend, and for the rest of my time under his care I sang it every Saturday night and looked forward to singing it. It was another one of the little things that seem almost infantile by themselves but provided a growing mass of tiny, essential props for my morale.

My Saturday-night sleep was long, dreamless, and a total escape. Stiff muscles on Sunday, but a vigorous walk in the yard and through my mental landscape and road map, and lots more accumulated kilometers. And then came another immense lift to my morale.

I had become aware that I had a neighbor in the next cell. I could hear whispered remarks from the guard at mealtime and the sound of a slot moved back and forth. That was the first indication of anyone in the adjacent cell, and I believe he must have just been moved in there. Then, on Sunday afternoon, while I sat on the toilet and worked away at

[a] fishbone, I heard a sound that gave my spirit a huge jolt of excitement. The simplest of sounds. A series of taps on the wall, clearly coming from the next cell.

I tapped back with my knuckles. *Tap, tap, tap.*

He tapped back. Three taps. There was a pause. I heard the peephole open and managed to get up in one motion and walk about concentrating on my fishbone.

Then there was a pause for his peephole. Then another series of taps, quite rapid, but distinctly spaced in double groups: 2, 4. Then 1, 5. Then 4, 3. Then 1, 1. And so on. At least, that's what I thought I heard at first. I knew Morse code well enough to recognize that this was not it. But it was a code, no mistaking. Then I remembered my book, *Political Prisoners in Tsarist Russia.* This must be the prison Morse! Damn! Why hadn't that rotten author explained the code! I began to answer in the same patterns, except that some of his groups were pretty long and I could not remember the entire sequence so I would just break down and send a whole series of staccato taps, or two taps and then two more. I was laughing out loud for joy. I had a companion! A fellow human being was next door, a fellow sufferer, someone to make common cause with, someone who would care and understand. I had no idea what his code was or whether it was even in Russian. But it was communication. I became totally absorbed in tapping, listening, tapping, laughing. I paid no attention to the peephole, forgot all about it. The slot burst open with an awful clang. The guard on duty was not friendly but not an extremely bad guy either. He just said in a no-nonsense way, "Ne polozheno!

And if you do it again, it will be hard punishment cells. Tapping is a very serious offense!" He glared at me to make sure I understood. I said, "I understand," and went over to my bunk and sat down. My heart was beating with excitement. I heard the slot in the cell next to me bang open and knew from the rumble of his voice that the guard was giving the same warning to my new friend. But I knew we could work it out, and I was ecstatic.

I spent some time training the guard with my hat. Then I went to work on the fishbone again and, being so full of high spirits, got an idea that seemed as though it might work. I split the end of the soft bone and twisted the two split ends around the point of a match. I thought that when it dried and hardened I could remove the match and I would then have a workable needle with an eye cemented together by natural bone glue. It took a day for the bone to dry, and when I looped a thread through the eye and started to work on a rip in my shirt, the needle held together. A small success that seemed a triumph. I had lost several buttons from my shirt. Seeing how hard and smooth the bread in my calendar had become, I pressed and molded some bread buttons and pierced holes in them. When they dried in a day or two, I polished them on the blanket until they were smooth as bone and sewed them on my shirt. The needle wore out after a while but it was a welcome task to make another.

My neighbor and I continued our blind correspondence. The next time the wind tunnel started up I tapped as hard as I could on the wall, between peepholes. I knew it could never be heard outside the cell. Back came the answer. Always in the groupings of two numbers. Now I realized that the same figure occurred over and over again like a musical theme. It went: 2, 4; 3, 6; 3, 2 (pause). Then 1, 3; 5, 2.

I tried returning the same pattern, as soon as I had it memorized. This set off a terrific rattle of taps. I realized that my neighbor thought I suddenly understood the code. I felt impotent and frustrated. I answered with a simple pair of taps. He must have understood. A simple double tap came back.

We found we could get away with tapping while the food was being distributed; that was the only time when the peephole was not opened every minute. In the evenings I began to realize that a new pattern was emerging. My neighbor would start with the familiar 2, 4; 3, 6; 3, 2 . . . 1, 3; 5, 2.

I would answer with a single tap. He must have taken that to mean *I don't understand.* Then he would begin the following pattern: 1, 1; 1, 2; 1, 3; 1, 4; 1, 5; 1, 6. Then a pause. Then 2, 1; 2, 2; 2, 3; 2, 4; 2, 5; 2, 6. Then a pause. Then 3, 1; 3, 2 and so on to 3, 6. Then it would be 4, 1 to 4, 6. Then 5, 1 to 5, 6. I knew there was some kind of key in this. I got out my remaining match stubs. I set them out on the blanket in the number groupings I had heard. My brain was slow and numb from sleeplessness. Something obvious as hell was there. I knew it. But I could not get it. I would answer back a single tap. *I do not understand.* And patiently he began again, 1, 1; 1, 2; right through the whole sequence.

We had to be very careful not to get caught.

Sitting on the toilet I found I could tap very quietly on the drainpipe, which branched through the wall into the next cell, and get a response. The toilet was to the right of the door, looking in from outside. The guard could not see my right hand down beside the iron cone, tapping ever so lightly.

My friend kept up his attempts at instruction during every meal, but in the morning he would just tap simple taps that corresponded to the rhythms and routine of the day. No code; just an acknowledgment that we were sharing the same experience. Two taps: *good morning*, as I came back from interrogation. (He was always there when I came back; he was not in interrogation then?) Two taps: *going for my walk now*, when they came to take him to exercise. Two taps: *I'm back*. Two little human bits of caring.

I continued to train the guards to believe I was awake under the shadow of the hat. I had to reach the point where they would not wait to see if I moved, where they would simply make a routine stop at the peephole and go on. Once that was established I could dare to try an extended sleep every day. By extended, I mean an hour or so.

Sidorov was trying to work up a satisfactory set of protocols on the information system within the United States Embassy. Sometimes he cuffed me pretty hard on the ears and made my head ring. But for a couple of weeks there was no more serious beating. I still often went out cold in the interrogation room, and then he would slap me awake and curse and yell. But for the time being he did not kick my slowly healing shins.

Almost every day now, I told myself the plot of a movie. A favorite was *13 Rue Madeleine*, a story of commandos and the Gestapo and parachuting into occupied France.

I held my own private screening several times. I found that each time I "saw" this movie I remembered more detail, and after a while I could almost have written out the screenplay.

I started lectures in world geography, calling up everything I could remember about rainfall, population, industry, vegetation, rivers, towns, political structure, and all the rest.

And I trained and trained the guards to think I was wide awake under the hat. Before long I began to give them their midterm tests and then their final exams. They all passed except that squat old bag, and I just gave up on her, but soon, with the rest, I could always get sleep in half-hour chunks, and with the young Komsomol I could sleep for two hours, which was as long as my back held out.

At this point I can predict, I think, what a reader of this page will feel. Relief. "He's got it made. It's all right now."

Part of this is what I felt. Relief, certainly, and a certainty that I was now going to survive. But there was a grimmer side to it. As soon as Sidorov started to beat me, I realized clearly that I was going to be in prison for a long time. I did not think in terms of specific periods, and I certainly did not think it would be for the rest of my life. But I knew it was not going to be over soon. I knew there would be more beatings and that I would suffer a lot. I knew I would have to train myself to meet that menace, and the knowledge made me feel numb in the heart. The two or three hours of light sleep I was able to steal each day barely kept me from caving in. I was constantly hungry. My weight dropped steadily. When they gave me back my hat, the hell I was living in became a hell I could survive, but it was still hell. I believe it was at that time that my eyes and my mouth began to settle into a grim cast which is still my normal expression when I am not excited or laughing, and even then I am told it lingers around my eyes. My iron mask never came off, and I can see that it never will.

3.

ELENA GLINKA

lena Glinka was a twenty-nine-year-old engineer
when she was arrested in 1950. Imprisoned for six
years, she returned to Moscow in 1956 and re-
enrolled at the shipbuilding institute where she had been
studying when she was taken away. From then on, in the
words of one of her fellow students, she "said nothing at all
about her life 'over there.'" Occasionally, she would remi-
nisce about some of the good people she had met, or about
those who helped her, but she did not describe in detail the
horrors she had experienced.

Perhaps her earlier reticence helps explain why the essay which follows, first published in the literary magazine
Neva in 1989, came as such a profound shock to Glinka's
friends and family and to Russian readers in general. Until
then stories of rape in the Gulag had been virtually taboo.
Although many had witnessed such atrocities, they rarely
mentioned them in published accounts. Glinka broke that
taboo for good with this essay, which describes a mass rape

of prisoners from one of the ships en route from the Pacific port of Vladivostok to Magadan, the "capital" city of the Kolyma peninsula, home of the notorious Kolyma camps. Although the account is written in the third person, one of the characters described is clearly herself.

Glinka's description of the phenomenon of mass rape has since been echoed by others, notably the Polish writer Janusz Bardach, who watched a group of criminal prisoners rip a hole in an interior wall of a Kolyma-bound ship in order to get at the female prisoners on the other side. In Bardach's account, "hundreds of men hung from the bed boards to view the scene, but not a single one tried to intervene." The mass rape on Bardach's ship ended only when the guards on the upper deck sprayed water into the hold below; the dead women were then dragged out and presumably thrown overboard. "Anyone who has seen Dante's hell," wrote another surviving prisoner, "would say that it was nothing beside what went on in that ship."

It is important to remember while reading the following account that although this scene certainly occurred "under the government flag, with government collusion," as Glinka writes, these outrages were not ordered by Moscow. According to the Gulag's own rules, transportation of prisoners was not supposed to be a form of punishment: convoy guards were explicitly told to ensure that prisoners arrived at camps healthy enough to work. But although the archives are full of reprimands, angry letters to commanders of convoy battalions who killed or starved too many prisoners in the course of transporting them east, in practice few were punished. Mass rapes may not have been ordered, in other words—but they were easily tolerated by convoy guards who did not care enough to stop them, and administrators who were far away. Some of that indifference is conveyed in this account by Glinka's carefully emotionless prose.

The Kolyma Tram

There was a saying in the camps: the Kolyma tram is something that runs you over, but maybe, just maybe, you might come out alive.

The sad fishing village of Bugurchan, a barely visible dot on the coast of Okhostk, consisted of five or six scattered log huts plus a pitiful town hall with three small windows and a flag—perhaps the village chairman had no spare red calico for a new one, who knows? At any rate that same bleached-out flag had probably flown over Bugurchan since long before the war. But the hammer and sickle in its corner still stood out as distinctly as the numbers on a prison jacket.

One day, a ship that regularly hauled supplies and workers to the villages and camps during summer navigation season brought in a holdful of female convicts, a "punishment brigade." They disembarked to shouts and obscenities and the barking of guard dogs, and were driven to the town hall, where the guard detail diligently counted heads—after which the chief guard ordered them to stay where they were and went off to find the sole local representative of

government authority, the village chairman, in order to officially transfer custody.

The group consisted mainly of those convicted of petty
crimes or workplace transgressions,[1] with a few hard cases
thrown in—pitiful creatures who had suffered a common
fate: parents executed or killed in the war; NKVD orphan-
ages; escape to the streets, poverty, and hunger until at some
point they were picked up for pilfering a potato or a carrot
from a shop counter. Branded as criminals, rejected by society, they soon turned into the genuine article. Among them
there were some recidivists, hardened criminals who in
camp slang were called *zhuchki,* "bugs." Now here they all
were, planted in front of the town hall, bickering with one
another, rifling through their bundles and pestering their
guards for cigarettes.

The camp authorities had tossed another ingredient
into this hash of ruined lives: three political prisoners convicted under Article 58.[2] One was an older woman, the
wife of a disgraced diplomat; the second was a middle-aged
seamstress; the third was a student from Leningrad.[3] None
had any record of defying or disrupting camp discipline—it
was just that the punishment brigade was thrown together
in a hurry and the number of troublemakers did not meet
the quota set out in the directive. So in order to make the

1. In Russian, *bytovichki.*
2. Article 58 was the legal statute under which political prisoners were
convicted.
3. Glinka was the student from Leningrad.

required head count, the authorities had included some "heavyweights": inmates who had been sentenced to twenty-five years.

"Women in Bugurchan!" The news spread like wildfire throughout the taiga, stirring the area up like an anthill. Within an hour men began flocking to the town hall—first the locals, then men from farther afield, some on foot, some on motorbikes. There were fishermen, geologists, fur trappers, a team of miners and their Party boss, and even some convicts, thieves and criminals who had bolted from their logging camp. As the men began to arrive, the zhuchki began to stir, buzzing, trading barbs—brassy prison slang heavily laced with obscenities.

The guard detail bellowed at the zhuchki to stay where they were and ordered the others to keep their distance; somewhere in the shouting was a threat that the militia had both dogs and firearms at their disposal and were ready to use them, but since almost all the men knew their way around the camps, they didn't push their luck (all the more so because someone had already sweetened the guards' mood with liquor). The guards didn't bother to chase them off completely, just yelled at their retreating backs, and settled themselves nearby.

The zhuchki were cadging loose tobacco and tea for brewing *chifir;*[4] they offered homemade tobacco pouches in trade. Most of the men had already stocked up on supplies

---

4. A form of strong tea with narcotic properties.

either at home or the village store. Over the women's heads, into the crowd, flew packs of cigarettes and packets of tea, chunks of bread, cans of food. Tossing a crust of bread to a famished prisoner was an act that suggested political unreliability, a punishable act if committed back *there*, in long-suffering Mother Russia; *there* one was supposed to patriotically lower one's eyes, walk on by, and forget. But here—perhaps because almost all the local men had a prison past—a different law prevailed. A group of fish salters and the one and only cooper in the village (already fairly drunk) had brought a parcel of cured salmon and proceeded to cut it up and toss the pieces to the female prisoners.

Worn down by seasickness and two hungry days in the hold, the women caught these handouts on the fly, hurriedly stuffed them into their mouths and swallowed without chewing. The zhuchki, coughing hoarsely, took long drags on their Belomors.[5] For a time, all was quiet. Then bottles began to clink, and several of the men, as if on command, retreated to one side and sat down to drink with the guard detail.

Sated, the women struck up a song, first "The Long Road," then "Sister," and the men replied with the famous camp song "Tsentralka."[6] After this group sing everyone perked up and began to mingle with no thought for the guards, who by now had shed their rifles, tied their dogs to

5. A cheap brand of cigarette named after the White Sea Canal, a Gulag camp in the 1930s.
6. "The Central Prison."

the trees, and were busy drinking hard with their chief and the village chairman.

But it was only the zhuchki, the criminal women, who showed much enthusiasm. The petty thieves and offenders who made up the majority of the brigade were quieter. They kept largely to themselves. Granted, they just as eagerly took the handouts; they entered into conversations, but they seemed somehow absent. Their thoughts were elsewhere; many were now doing short time, and, unlike the politicals, they did not face exile after camp. The short-time zhuchki also were counting down the days, and although none of them had anywhere to go or anyone to turn to, and the idea of freedom frightened some (automatically dooming them to helplessness and indifference to their own fate), the prospect of future sorrows seemed not to exist. Freedom was freedom, that was the main thing, and that itself gave them hope. The political "heavyweights" had no hope at all; the Gulag had swallowed them forever.

The three politicals sat apart from the crowd: the student, the seamstress, and the wife of an "enemy of the people." They already knew the purpose behind the whole debauch, the carousing with the guards; they had realized this long before, one by one, the soldiers passed out dead drunk, and before the men, whooping and hollering, rushed the women and began to haul them into the building, twisting their arms, dragging them through the grass, brutally beating any who resisted. The tethered dogs yipped and barked and strained at their leashes.

The men knew their business; the operation was co-ordinated and confident. One group pulled up the benches nailed to the floor and tossed them onto the stage; a second group boarded up the windows; still others rolled in small kegs and set them upright along the walls, then hauled in water by the bucket; a fourth group brought grain alcohol and fish. That done, they nailed planks crosswise over the doors, spread out whatever rags or blankets they had at hand—padded vests, bedrolls, mats—and began throwing the women to the floor. A line of about a dozen men formed by each woman, and so began the mass rapes known as the "Kolyma tram." They were by no means rare in the Stalin era, and everywhere they happened in the same way—under the government flag, with government collusion.

I offer this documentary account to all the die-hard Stalinists who to this day do not want to believe that the lawlessness and sadism of these reprisals were consciously encouraged by their idol. Let them at least for a moment imagine their wives, daughters, and sisters in that Bugurchan brigade; after all, it was purely by accident that we, not they, ended up there.

It was rape on command: a "tram driver" would raise his arms and shout "Mount up!" Then at the command "Show's over!" the man would pull away, reluctantly ceding his place to the next in line, who was standing at full attention in all senses of the word.

The dead were dragged away by their feet and piled next to the doors; the survivors were doused with water from the buckets and revived. Then the lines formed up again.

But Bugurchan wasn't the biggest tram; it was just an average, "middleweight" car, so to speak . . .

By nightfall the men were all dead to the world; some occasionally got up and stumbled around, tripping over sleeping bodies, gulping water from the barrels, puking, then flopping back down to the floor or onto the nearest victim.

Was there ever anything like this even in those dream-times when we first raised our front legs off the ground and began to walk upright, when our primitive ancestors lived by animal and herd instinct alone? I don't think so.

The beautiful and stately seamstress took the heaviest blow during this first pass of the Kolyma tram. The wife of the enemy of the people was spared the worst of it thanks to her age: her "partners" were for the most part impotent old men. Only one of the three was relatively lucky. The miners' Party boss chose her for himself, took her for both days. The miners respected him: he was fair, he was straight with them, man to man, politically reliable, morally strong. They accepted him as their leader, and his ride on the tram somehow justified and united them all: just like us, they are, our *politruk*[7] and our state. Out of respect for him none of his crew even approached the student, and the Party boss even gave her a little gift—a new comb, the rarest of things in the camps.

Unlike the rest of the women, she didn't end up screaming, fighting back, trying to pull away: she thanked God that she'd become the property of just one.

7. Political commissar of a military unit.

4.

KAZIMIERZ ZAROD

In the photograph which precedes the introduction to his memoir, *Inside Stalin's Prisons,* Kazimierz Zarod is walking down a prosperous Warsaw boulevard dressed in a wool coat, wool scarf, and hat. Young and handsome, he strides beside an equally young and handsome woman, also wearing a wool coat, hers with a fur collar. Twenty-six years old when the war broke out, Zarod was a Polish civil servant and an army reservist. Along with many others, he fled from Warsaw to eastern Poland after the Germans invaded the country on September 1, 1939. He was then trapped there on September 17, when the Soviet Union invaded Poland from the east. Arrested as a "refugee" in what was no longer Poland but had been named "Soviet West Ukraine," Zarod was considered highly suspicious because of his fluent Russian (his family had lived in Russia before the Revolution). After his interrogation, Zarod was sent to a Siberian forestry camp, which he knew only as "Labor Corrective Camp No. 21."

The story of Zarod's arrest was in some ways typical: between the Soviets' invasion of Poland in 1939 and the Germans' invasion of the Soviet Union in 1941, more than 400,000 Poles were arrested, of which some 108,000 were sent directly to the Gulag (the rest went to exile villages). The story of Zarod's release was not unusual either: in 1941, following the German invasion, the Soviet Union and Poland concluded a temporary truce, and Stalin agreed to allow a Polish army to be formed on Soviet territory under the command of General Władysław Anders. Zarod marched out of Russia with what came to be called Anders's Army. Traveling via Tehran, Bombay (Mumbai), and Cape Town, he wound up in Britain, where he joined the Royal Air Force Bomber Command. After the war he stayed in England, married an Englishwoman, and taught Polish and Russian to two generations of British soldiers. He published his memoirs in 1990, after his retirement.

Zarod was not a literary writer, and his book contains few rhetorical flourishes. Nevertheless, it is extraordinarily useful precisely because he focuses on things that "better" writers often ignored: what prisoners ate, where they lived, where they worked. In the selection that follows, Zarod describes, in his straightforward manner, a typical prisoner's day.

A Day in Labor Corrective Camp No. 21

At 3:00 A.M. each morning reveille was beaten out on a triangle. Dressing was unnecessary as we slept in our clothes for warmth. Tumbling off the hard wooden shelf on which I had spent the night, I joined the queue which was forming near the water bucket in one corner of the hut. By this time we had all acquired soup containers—a round tin with two holes punched near the top through which string or a narrow piece of material or wire was threaded—and, filling the container, I splashed my face with a few handfuls, keeping the rest to drink, as water was scarce. We had no towels; a piece of rag or one's coat sleeve had to suffice. Soap was a great luxury, the piece we were issued with once a month being so small that we kept it to use in the evenings when we returned from work, really dirty.

By 3:30 A.M. we were supposed to be in the middle of the square, standing in ranks of fives, waiting to be counted. The guards often made mistakes, and then there had to be a second count. On a morning when it was snowing this was a long, cold, agonizing process. If the guards were wide awake and concentrating, the count usually took about thirty minutes, but if they miscounted, we could stand for anything up to an hour.

The guards having satisfied themselves that the right number of bodies was present on the square, the brigadier (foreman) was dispatched to collect the bread for the day. From the beginning we were split into working parties of thirty men—a "brigade"—each brigade having its foreman, or brigadier. He was nominally responsible for the group of thirty men. His duties included the distribution of the day's ration of bread, supervision of the group, and allocation of work in the forest. At night, the day's work done, he reported to the office with the figures of work accomplished by each man during the day. These returns handed in every evening by the brigadier were the difference between life and death for prisoners. The amount of work done determined the amount of bread each prisoner received on the following day. A hundred percent return—a physical impossibility for most men (although there were those who managed to bribe the brigadier with tobacco or other smuggled delicacies, to juggle the figures, a very risky business as if caught the brigadier stood to lose his privileged position)— earned 900 grams of bread (about 2 lbs). On average, at least in the early months of captivity while they still remained fairly healthy, men could accomplish 75 percent and earned 800 grams [28 ounces] of bread; 50 percent, 700 grams [25 ounces], under 50 percent, 300 grams [10 1/2 ounces]. Made of rye which had not been thoroughly cleaned, it was literally "black" bread because the bran left in it colored the bread black and made its texture coarse. The source of life, it was carefully hoarded through the day. A little with the breakfast soup, a few bites during the short break at dinnertime (midday), more with the soup in the evening to stave off the pangs of hunger in the freezing night.

If a prisoner stole clothes, tobacco, or almost anything else and was discovered, he could expect a beating from his fellow prisoners, but the unwritten law of the camp—and I have heard from men from other camps that it was the same everywhere—was that a prisoner caught stealing another's bread earned a death sentence! It might not happen straight away, but by some means or other he would be killed—an "accident" was not difficult to arrange in the forest.

There was one other duty the brigadier had each day, and that was to decide who should be the duty man (*dnyevalny*). This was a job much coveted as it meant staying in the camp all day to tend the fire in the barrack, sweeping the dirt floor, filling the water buckets, and various other simple jobs. The job of dnyevalny was supposed to be allocated on a rota system, but in practice the brigadier was instructed to pick the dnyevalny for the day from the men in his group who were not strong, or ill and therefore weak. Over the months an element of bribery entered into it, and men fought tooth and nail about who should be chosen.

Having received our ration of bread each morning from the brigadier we joined a queue outside the cookhouse, this time for soup. There was a relatively large dining hall with rough wooden tables and benches next door to the cookhouse, which accommodated about three hundred men at a time, and sometimes if there was room I ate my breakfast as well as my evening meal there, but more often than not I carried my soup tin back to the barrack hut and ate there, sitting on my bunk.

Distributing food and the eating of it with so many men took quite a long time and it was usually about 5:30 A.M. when we were ready for work. The really old and seriously ill were allocated jobs inside the camp. They worked in the cookhouse, the ration store, sauna; stoked the central heating plant; acted as barbers, hospital orderlies, administration personnel, bookkeepers, accountants, clerks, copytypists (there were only two typewriters in the camp to cope with the immense amount of paperwork), cleaners, sweepers, transport workers, etc. A small party of prisoners was dispatched twice a week, heavily guarded, to the nearest village, Syemyonovka, about seventeen kilometers [ten and a half miles] distant. It was the last "station" where food was deposited for collection by men from a few camps in the area. Traveling in horse-drawn carts, these prisoners collected barrels of salt fish, black bread, and vegetables, and, for the use of the soldiers and such civilian personnel as were in the camp, white bread, cereals, oil, margarine, flour, sugar, tea, coffee and condensed milk, etc.

For the rest of us, day after day, labor in the forest. Our departure each morning was bizarre. Among so many prisoners there were represented all the professions, and very soon after our arrival the commandant had organized a "band" of musicians. Some were professionals, others amateur, but together they made quite good music. Each morning the "band" stood near the gate playing military-style music, and we were exhorted to march out "strongly and happily" to our day's work. Having played until the end of the column had passed through the gate, the musicians abandoned their instruments and, tacking themselves onto the end of the column, joined the workers walking into the forest.

When we arrived at whatever site was being worked, the first task for two of the men was to build a fire for the guards. We worked, cutting as many trees down as possible, trimming and stacking the wood in the prescribed way. Work continued until midday, when if we were lucky in our guard and he was one of the kinder and more humane ones, he would arrange for small parties to take a break in turn, which meant that we could get nearer the fire while we rested and ate our bread. Work continued through the afternoon and early evening, until at 6:00 P.M. the guard took out his whistle and blew it.

All the tools we used were potential weapons, and the guards were very much aware of this, as were we. As the ranks of men fell into formation to begin the long walk back to the camp each night, the guards walked up and down the line reminding us that any attempt to break ranks would earn a bullet.

Carrying the heavy saws and choppers, ropes slung over shoulders, we straggled rather than marched back toward camp, where all the forestry equipment was stored for the night in large huts outside the gates. The equipment put away safely for the night, we entered the camp and were allowed one hour in which to wash, rest, and collect our evening soup. At 9:00 P.M. we once more stood in ranks of five on the barrack square while the guards counted (if we were lucky) and re-counted (if we were not); and so, finally, merciful sleep.

5.

ANATOLY ZHIGULIN

Though his childhood was marked by war and his adolescence by arrest and incarceration, Anatoly Zhigulin retained a powerful nostalgia for an older, simpler, holier Russia throughout his life. He was born in 1930 in a small Russian village, and an idyllic image of what Russia had been—and should be—permeated the poetry for which he became famous after his return from the camps in 1954. At times that nostalgia also seeps into *Black Stones*, the memoir he wrote of the five years he spent in the Gulag.

Though Zhigulin's poetry was officially published during the Soviet period, *Black Stones* appeared only in the late 1980s following the introduction of Mikhail Gorbachev's perestroika reforms. The book became a best seller in Russia not only because of Zhigulin's portrayal of his Gulag experience but also because he described a forgotten generation of teenagers, young men and women who came of age in the late 1940s. Inspired by a burst of postwar idealism, some had formed sincere but amateurish political groups.

As a result, these young half-rebels were arrested for "anti-Stalinist activities."

To be arrested for crimes against the state was not unusual at that time, of course: anyone who allegedly told a joke about Stalin, or even listened to a joke about Stalin, could be sent to the Gulag. But Zhigulin and his friends, like similar groups scattered around Russia, really had engaged in what might be called anti-Stalinist activities. These were the efforts of schoolchildren: often they did nothing more than form cells and write leaflets, copying the tactics of the Bolsheviks they were reading about in history classes. The bravery of these protodissidents, at a time when few adults dared talk about anything political, was notable nevertheless.

Zhigulin's memoir is also famous for its account of the camps in the period following World War II, when the prisoners had become savvier and better organized than their prewar counterparts. Many of them were former Red Army soldiers or partisans, who were more than capable of coming up with ways to avoid death through overwork and starvation. Zhigulin himself worked in many parts of the Gulag, including the uranium mines of Kolyma. What interested him most, however, were the people he met and the methods they used to cope with the bizarre conditions in which they found themselves. In the selection printed here he discusses some of the ways in which prisoners manipulated their situation in order to survive: by feigning illness, seeking transfers to "easier" camps, cheating on work norms.

He also reflects on the phenomenon of soldiers shooting at prisoners in order to collect rewards for "preventing escapes" and describes a few "rare" moments of joy. Zhigulin was one of those writers who understood that life went on inside the camps and that prisoners had a wide range of experiences, not merely suffering.

On Work

ANGINA

In spite of the relatively light work, I was on my last legs. So once, after a hot twelve-kilometer [seven-and-a-half-mile] sprint to our log site, I went to the water barrel. I broke the thick layer of ice with a wooden ladle and drank my fill of water so cold that it numbed my teeth and throat. Then I took a few deep breaths of that forty-below air. By evening my throat hurt terribly; it was painful to swallow; I felt feverish. After waiting for a long time in the long line for the doctor, I was admitted to our small, five-bed infirmary. What the doctor found was a monstrous case of follicular angina and a temperature of 40-plus [over 104]. That very long line had consisted mostly of prisoners suffering from malnutrition, who of course should also have been admitted as inpatients. But malnutrition was not on the official list of recognized illnesses; otherwise the camp administrators would have had to hospitalize two or three hundred people at a time.

But I, aside from being dystrophic, was obviously and seriously ill. Oh, those wonderful ten or twenty days in the hospital! Food for the patients was prepared separately and resembled the real thing. The soup consisted of more than just potatoes; there was cabbage too, and some greens. I just lay there; I could rest. It was clean, warm, cozy. And every day, several times a day, I retreated to the relatively warm toilet and knocked the ice off the windowpanes: I sucked on the bigger pieces to keep my angina going. There were no antibiotics; all that we had was streptocid.[1] Prisoners could not stay in the infirmary more than ten days, and on the thirteenth day I was discharged and sent back to the barracks with a three-day leave from work.

LAYING TRACK IN WINTER

I was assigned to the track-laying crew after my bout with angina. Digging ditches, building roadbeds. First, however, came the survey work. Breaking down the curves and all that. I worked at practically every job on that crew. The worst part was digging the ditches because there was no way to manipulate the work norms. All you could do to conserve your strength was look for lighter work or some other way to meet quotas: shovel snow, clear trees, light fires to melt the permafrost, do pickax work; you could pad the distance

1. Possibly sulfa.

dirt had to be hauled by wheelbarrow. But meeting the "dirt quota" per person was impossible. What were we to do? People were growing weaker by the day, people were dying. They had to be saved. Meanwhile, the free workers and the camp administrators were demanding full volume—X amount of dirt dug, X amount of fill. Write it up however you like—just give us the dirt. Easy to measure and to check.

Our crew boss, Sergei Zakharchenko, was a savvy man. A sapper. He'd landed in camp severely contused after blowing up a bridge to stop an enemy advance—hadn't managed to get far enough away from his own charge. He understood that the process of saving people began with plotting the route; Zakharchenko had a knack for laying out roadbeds that required almost no digging.

Coming up with the fill was no problem. We had lookouts standing watch at both ends of the work zone; they would send a signal (a certain number of knocks on the rails) when the bosses were on their way. We'd pile it high. On either side of the roadbed we would clear off the snow and dig up one layer of soil. Everything looked fine— wheelbarrows standing there full of clay. Then we'd toss on some snow. Pack it down. Toss in branches, toss in the needles from the tops of the trees. Then more and more snow. We'd pile it high. Some more dirt on top. Half a meter [twenty inches]. Tamp it down. Hard? Hard! It's below zero. The snow, the needles, the branches, the dirt all frozen into a solid monolith. The ties and the rails laid on top. When would our little dodge come to light? Maybe eight or ten months from now, and by that time we'll be gone. We'll be working on another branch line in another place.

But meanwhile, people will have been saved, people will have been fed. Other convicts will do penance for our sins (our shoddy work), will have to dump more dirt, more gravel; but they won't bother to dig the snow, the pine needles, the branches out of the railbed. They'll just fill in the sinkholes where the railbed has shifted. Shifting is a normal thing in winter. It's even anticipated, planned for. And meanwhile, where will we be? By then, probably, in Kolyma. At least that's where many of us ended up.

But as spring came on, so did mass starvation. That's when I resolved on one last desperate act.

"SAMORUB"

This was the term we coined for taking an ax to ourselves to get out of work. The penalty for this was severe—*samorub*[2] equaled sabotage. As it happened, at the time I was out working on repairs to a skid road; I was wearing winter foot cloths and boots. The road lay over a bog that was thawing and sucking down the road, despite the freezing weather. I was shaping new ties to replace the rotted ones. The usual routine. The new ties lay alongside the old ones, parallel to the rails. Across from me, on the other side of the tracks, sat a soldier with an automatic, warming himself at the camp-

2. Prison slang for a self-inflicted wound.

fire. I forget his name, but we were from the same part of the country. He'd been born somewhere around Sagunov, not far from Podgorny.

We chatted about where we'd grown up; he shared some tobacco. The sun was shining. Our little fire burned bright and smokeless. I was slowly dressing the log, swinging the ax back and forth between it and my left foot. Just a bit more to the left and so much for my foot. I was aiming for the gap between my big toe and second toe. This would be hard to pull off. I had to calculate the force of the swing so that the cut wouldn't be too deep. I kept chopping, gradually moving my foot closer and closer (never looking at the soldier or looking around). A few more weak chops and finally (for better or worse) the ax blade bit hard into my boot just up by that toe. It truly hurt and naturally I yelped, dropped the ax, and started swearing a blue streak.

My soldier saw the whole thing, and in his mind it was purely an accident, a bad swing. Blood was oozing fairly thickly out of the gash in my boot. I couldn't walk, and four of my fellow convicts carried me back to the yard as my countryman with the automatic strode alongside. When the report reached the commander, the guard said yes, I'd been working along just fine. No samorub—pure accident. The wound in my foot was wide, but not very deep. The doctor put in four stitches, inserted a drainage tube, and issued me a pair of crutches.

"OK, you're done. You've got a couple of months off—lucky man."

The wound took a long time to heal because I was constantly stripping off the bandage and sprinkling all sorts of crap into the cut—obviously when the doctor wasn't looking. I lolled around the yard on crutches for a good two months during the worst time of the year.

THE HUNT

This cannibalistic sport was especially popular with the guard details and sentries at Camp No. 031. But it flourished everywhere throughout the Gulag given the right conditions: small groups of convicts out in the woods, in the field; automatic weapons; close range; someone easy to shoot.

There was a system of incentives for guards who prevented or interrupted escapes. Shoot a runner—get a new stripe on your uniform, home leave, a bonus, a medal. No doubt biology was at work here as well—the aggression that comes naturally to young males. Moreover, hatred for the prisoners was inculcated in them from the start. The prisoners were *vlasovtsy*,[3] they were S.S., they were traitors and spies. Guards were perverted both by the absolute power they were given and by the weapons they so longed to use. Convicts were generally shot down either by very young soldiers or by hardened sadists and murderers. . . . One of the convoy detail would pick a victim and begin to stalk him. The guard would wheedle, persuade, try to lure

3. Soviet soldiers who collaborated with German forces during World War II.

the victim over the line. Unless a smart and savvy crew boss had warned the victim ahead of time, the deception worked. The soldier would say, "Hey! You! Go get me that little log to sit on!"

"But sir, it's off limits!"

"Not a problem. You have my permission. Move, go!"

The prisoner steps over the line. One quick burst of fire, and he's dead. Typical. Banal.

Sometimes the guards and sentries would actually order their victims to step over the line, or just shove or chase them out, the better to shoot them. A guard was authorized to order a convict to cross the cordon. He was also authorized to mow that same man down.

A person can sense when he's about to be shot. There's a certain feeling in the air. I sensed it several times during my stay at No. 031. Once was when Sergei Zakharchenko's repair crew was sent out to a work site. The guards drove in stakes topped by little white planks to mark off the perimeter: up the tracks, down the tracks, on both sides of the roadbed. Anything outside those stakes was off limits. One soldier suddenly barked, "Hey, you, go cut down that little tree over there. It's in my way, I can't see the track line."

Zakharchenko overheard and thundered out, "Zhigulin! Not a step outside! He'll kill you! Everybody down! Lie down on the ties! Do *not* follow the guards' orders! Stay down! Wait for the brass!"

There were five guards in the detail. The man in charge, their sergeant major, caught on right away, and didn't

challenge Zakharchenko. He pulled out his revolver, fired a
few shots into the air, then called in his superiors. The officers came, took away the guard's automatic, and sent him
off to the brig. But that sort of happy ending was rare.

RARE JOYS

With the arrival of the new commandant, life in No. 031
became easier. I began receiving parcels from home. Sergei
Zakharchenko brought me back into his crew. There were
about twelve or fifteen men in the brigade, the railroad
maintenance crew, "Maintenance" for short. That spring was
short, and then it was summer.

Sometimes people ask me whether there were ever any
good times in the camps, ever a good mood.

Of course there were. The soul always seeks joy, yearns
for it. Not all our bright days or bright months had to do
with receiving letters or packages or the like. There were
good, even joyful moments that had nothing to do with material comforts. Of course there was an indirect connection,
a natural one.

My best time in the camps came at the start of my second year, when I was part of Sergei Zakharchenko's crew.

We would march out of the gates early in the morning.
We weren't the first out, though. The felling and skidding
crews left first. They had farther to go and backbreaking
work to do in a single day. Not like us. We weren't in any
hurry.

So finally, when the crowd at the guardhouse dispersed, big Lomakin, the dispatcher, would boom: "Maintenance! Zakharchenko! Move out!"

He would usually throw in a few unprintable phrases—no insult intended. Just for the sake of form. We walked through the gates, where we were met by our usual guard detail. The soldier who had pegged me for shooting was long gone. After spending some time in solitary in the brig, he'd been transferred to a mental hospital. The underboss and his rosy-cheeked helper, both western Ukrainians, picked up our tools—sledgehammers, wrenches, axes, saws—and we were on our way. Ahead of us, behind us, alongside us, walked our four guards (sometimes five), peacefully puffing on their little cigars. Zakharchenko was good at dealing with them; they respected him and therefore us.

The taiga was beautiful in those early morning hours. Close to the camp it was hacked, mutilated. Stumps jutted out of the ground; blackened, half-burned waste wood lay everywhere. Great yellow sandpits. But once we left the clearcut we would come into virgin taiga, where the pines, each more choice than the next, towered like a wall of bronze. The sun had just risen. Great drops of dew shone on the blue rails and the grayish ties, and the tops of the pines were golden in the sun. Cool, fair, clear everywhere. Chipmunks occasionally scurried across our path—a sign of good luck. It was easy walking along the railway tracks, feeling the weight of the sledgehammer on our shoulders, the polished handle smoothed by our rough hands. A good mood, a lively mood, and I would drift away . . .

And suddenly instead of a hammer I was carrying a rifle. And all of Siberia was burning; the camps were in revolt. And we were not a work crew, we were a platoon led by a seasoned officer, Sergei Zakharchenko. And we were going to free our comrades. Just around the corner was Camp No. 6, and shots would ring out . . .

"Citizen boss, stop here."

Zakharchenko's voice would bring me back to reality.

"We need to stop here."

We'd stop for half an hour. We'd replace a rotten tie, drive in some spikes, and head on down the line. We'd scramble over skid roads, up and down gullies and embankments, over wooden bridges with hardwood supports. And around every turn, over every rise, one far vista after another would unfold—the endless reaches of the taiga, shades of blue, purple, and smoky green.

6.

NINA GAGEN-TORN

Perhaps because she was an ethnographer by profession, Nina Gagen-Torn's descriptions of her fellow Gulag inmates have an unusual sharpness. Born in Saint Petersburg in 1900, Gagen-Torn was the daughter of a respected physician, a Russified Swede. This fact may have saved her life: upon her arrival at one camp, a doctor inspecting the prisoners asked her whether her father was Ivan Gagen-Torn, his former professor. When she said yes, he immediately declared that she was "ill," plucked her out of the brigade of women being marched off to work, and sent her to rest in the camp hospital.

Arrested in 1936, Gagen-Torn served two terms in the Gulag, from 1936 to 1942 in Kolyma, and from 1947 to 1952 in Mordovia. Such double arrests were common: anyone who had already served a prison term for a political crime remained suspicious, and when repressive measures were tightened in 1947, at the beginning of the Cold

War, hundreds of thousands of freed prisoners found
themselves once again behind barbed wire. Gagen-Torn
thus spent twelve years in prison camps. During that time
she composed dozens of verses, some of which were subse-
quently published. In the camps, she was known as a poet.
Outside the camps, she was a respected ethnographer and
historian.

The selection that follows is from Gagen-Torn's memoirs, *Memoria,* published in 1995, and comes from her second, postwar camp term. It shows both her poetic and her
ethnographic talents to good effect. Gagen-Torn describes
the phenomenon of faith in the camps—not only religious
faith but faith in communism and faith in nationalism as
well. Gagen-Torn herself was not a believer and thus treats
the subject dispassionately. But deep religious, political, or
patriotic belief was a source of strength for many in the
camps. In a world in which so much seemed arbitrary, faith
of various kinds gave inmates a reason to stay alive. Religious and national communities stuck together in the
camps and members helped one another obtain better jobs
and food. Many prisoners have written about the need they
felt during their years in the camps to have some kind of
goal, something which would make sense of their otherwise nonsensical experience: faith could provide such a
purpose.

On Faith

In this chapter I would like to write about those people who believed—those who, thanks to their faith, were never broken.

First of all there were the "Lenin loyalists," as they called themselves when I first encountered them in Kolyma. They readily acknowledged their ties to the Trotskyite opposition, and unfailingly pressed their demands. First among these was the publication of Lenin's deathbed letter, which Stalin had suppressed, thereby violating the principle of democracy within the Party.[1]

They believed that Stalin had turned the dictatorship *of* the proletariat into a dictatorship *over* the proletariat, that he had set a reign of terror in motion, that collectivization carried out by force and the wholesale enslavement of the peasantry had not advanced the cause of socialism, that the tactics of the Party as led by Stalin discredited the very idea of communism.

Only the blood of the Communist martyrs willing to do battle with the Stalinist line could save the Communist ideal. The Lenin loyalists were willing martyrs. They were driven through the streets of Vladivostok on their way from exile to the Kolyma camps, roughly a hundred of them, singing as they marched: "You fell victim to the fateful strife /

---

1. In the 1920s and 1930s Trotskyites were systematically arrested and sent to the Gulag. The letter referred to here was written by Lenin at the end of his life warning the Party against the machinations of Stalin.

to undying love for the people." The guards beat them with rifle butts, but the singing never stopped. They were herded into the ship's hold, but even from there the songs resounded. On landing in Kolyma, they declared a hunger strike and demanded "political conditions," which meant the right to send and receive letters, to read, and to be housed separately from the common criminals.[2] On the fifteenth day of the strike the prison authorities began to force-feed them. The prisoners resisted. On the ninetieth day the administration promised to meet their demands. The hunger strike ended. With the promise of a change in conditions they were split up and assigned to a number of different lagpunkts.[3] But later, gradually, all were brought back to Magadan and sent to the fearsome prison nicknamed "Vaskov's House."[4] New charges were brought. They knew that they would be shot, but again they went willingly. These were courageous people. No doubt all of them perished, but all had kept their faith, doing battle for communism as they understood it.

Other keepers of the faith were the nationalists from the newly annexed republics: the Baltics and Western

2. In tsarist Russia, political prisoners had special rights not granted to criminal prisoners. In the early years of the Soviet Union the Bolsheviks also granted these rights to their political opponents, but Stalin took them away.

3. An individual camp unit. There could be dozens, even hundreds, of lagpunkts within a single camp system.

4. The local prison was named after one of the first Magadan commanders.

Ukraine.[5] Although there were quite a few true activists in the camps, I rarely ran into them. At Lagpunkt No. 10, guards frisking a group of young Lithuanian women found pamphlets: songs in Lithuanian decorated by a vignette depicting an oak branch with acorns, a symbol of Lithuanian independence. The barracks were rife with whispers: "Found them out . . . celebrate Lithuania Day . . . confiscated everything . . . taken away . . . security tighter . . . no paper anymore . . . what will happen to those girls? New charges . . . poor things . . . high price."

Once I did meet a Ukrainian nationalist, a spare, thin woman with a burning gaze who refused to speak anything other than Ukrainian, and only with other Ukrainians. Given the number of Ukrainians in the camps, this wasn't particularly unusual. What made people notice her was her passion and intensity. It was clear that she was uninterested in food or everyday survival; it was clear that not for an instant did she ever forget that she was in enemy captivity. There came a day when she decided to demonstrate this.

It was a weekend. We were all preoccupied with our own affairs: mending, sewing, straightening our bunks. A low hum hung over the barracks.

A ringing voice suddenly cut through the hum.

5. The independent states of Lithuania, Latvia, and Estonia, along with territories that had previously been part of Poland, were annexed to the Soviet Union following World War II. The Polish territories became known as Western Ukraine and Western Belarus.

"Ladies!" she shouted from the middle of the hut. "To-day is the birthday of Stepan Bandera![6] Long live Stepan! *Khai zhive Pan Stepan!*"

A hush fell. Heads popped down from the upper bunks.

"*Khai zhive Pan Stepan! Khai zhive Nenko Ukraina!*" she shouted even louder. No response. She waved one hand in disgust and ran out. A few hours later she was marched off to the cooler . . . Where they shipped her next I don't know.

More visible, and more noticeable, were the various religious faiths. At times there was a tragic aura about these groups; at times they seemed merely grotesque. I have already described the nuns of Lagpunkt No. 6. At Lagpunkt No. 10 the Sisters were herded into a single barrack and forbidden contact with other prisoners. They themselves never sought any. At certain hours of the day hymns sounded from their barrack; otherwise silence reigned. Their steadfastness became abundantly clear when one very ill woman was called in: "You're being processed out. Pick up your documents, shove off home."

She calmly looked at them and said, "I do not recognize your authority. Your state is unholy, your passport bears the stamp of the Antichrist. I want none of it. Once I am freed you will just jail me again. Why should I leave?" She turned on her heel and headed back to the barracks. In her mind she was free; only her body was captive.

6. Stepan Bandera (1909–59) was a Ukrainian nationalist leader who led a powerful anti-Soviet partisan movement during World War II.

How did the women on work detail regard the nuns? Many carped at them: "We work—they don't! But they still get their bread! All our work . . . fine bunch of saints they are!" Others took a neutral stance—"not our business." Yet others handed them alms on the sly. They would tuck a package into the hem of a skirt and sneak into the nuns' hut, or would beckon one of them around a corner. Bowing low, they would say, "Take this, Sisters, in Christ's name . . . it's from home, not here . . ." The Sister would bow low in reply: "Christ be with you." And she would hide it in turn.

The Sisters were staunch in their observance, Old Believers whose traditions and conduct had been forged over centuries. It was as if we were in the presence of the old faith depicted more profoundly than Melnikov-Pechersky ever could.[7]

The range of religious beliefs was astonishing. Each version of each faith had its true believers and a set of hangers-on. In the summertime you could see them all in the corner of the camp we called the "park." Every birch tree was a chapel of sorts.

Between seven and eight in the morning, the guards' vigilance dulled a bit: breakfast was over, work details were being assigned, barracks were searched and inspected, the shift was about to change. They had their hands full.

---

7. The Old Believers are a Russian Orthodox sect that split away from the church in the seventeenth century as a protest against liturgical reform. The writer Pavel Melnikov-Pechersky (1818–83) described life in the Russian provinces and among the Old Believers.

The very time for morning prayer in the park.

The Russian Orthodox gather under one tree. Under another stand the "westerners," the Uniates. Then there are the Baptists and the Subbotniki.[8] Two Catholics find their own corner, and under the scornful gaze of the rest of the worshipers, begin praying in Latin. The Orthodox are singing the midday liturgy and the Uniates are saying, "That sounds like ours." They too kneel, raise their hands, palms together in the Catholic fashion, and begin praying.

"That looks like us," says Katya Golovanova, the head of the Russian Orthodox group. "Very much like us . . . but why bother to put your hands together? Then again everybody prays in their own way . . . we are all equal in the eyes of the Lord. Their singing is nice."

Katya herself had a wonderful voice; she was a fine singer. The Uniates were happy that she liked their singing. The churches were coming together.

The Baptists did not approve of songs; they thought hymns or liturgies unnecessary. They would chant poetry, often improvising it. They had their own leader, Sister Annushka, who interpreted the Gospel for them. The Subbotniki would sit on a single bench, discussing religion.

8. Uniates, also called "Greek Catholics," are an Eastern branch of Catholicism. Although they follow the Western pope, their rites and liturgy have more in common with Orthodoxy. The Subbotniki are a Russian Christian sect that follows many of the tenets of Judaism, including keeping the Sabbath on Saturday.

It was not until the camps that I realized that the Sub-botniki, the "Judaizing Christians" whom Ivan the Terrible had sought to destroy, still existed. This sect had outlived all the tsars. Its members regarded all tsars with contempt. They believed that the monarchy had conspired with the church to distort the word of God, had deceived the common folk by various designs, had renounced the only book given by God himself—the Old Testament. Their accusation: "In the Bible it is said—Remember the Sabbath day! But the lords and masters went and invented Sunday! A lie! And who wrote the Gospels? People wrote the Gospels. But the Bible comes from God. We must hold to the Bible: all the prophecies are there if you understand them rightly."

The Subbotniki debated with the Baptists, whose tree stood nearby. Young women reared by the Komsomol would sometimes join in. "Girls, you're talking foolishness!" they exhorted. "Some people have one God, others have another. But who's ever laid eyes on any of them? Nobody. Telescopes have explored the sky, pilots have crisscrossed it—nobody's seen a thing."

"Daughters," replied Sister Annushka. "God is a force unseen, like love. Can you feel love with your hands?"

"Of course," the girls replied. "Love is visible through works. Anyone can see it. But here there's so much injustice! How can God permit that, if he exists?"

Once I accidentally provided Sister Annushka with a very convincing argument. I had been talking about color blindness, about people who cannot tell green from red; their eyes are made that way, and they cannot see every color.

Annushka's face shone: "Now that's what science can show us! So we see the world not in its essence, but only as much of it as has been revealed to us. Some see more, some see less. There are people who cannot tell green from red, and there are people who can see the unseeable! And you know, I've heard that there's some kind of waves: sound waves, light waves—how does that work?"

I explained. This too was turned to some advantage in the debates—the news spread. The Subbotniki scurried up to ask whether it was true, then left, shaking their heads. In the barracks Katya Golovanova sidled up next to me and, straightening her white headscarf, quietly asked, "I heard that you were telling people about some sort of rays? They (by this she meant the Baptists) are twisting that their way."

For several days the discussion went on, as representatives of the various churches left their separate birches to talk with one another. This could have taken a dangerous turn: the guards might notice people gathering. Those same young girls saved the day.

"Attention, ladies!" they shouted. "Guard!"

And instantly the "park" emptied. The believers scattered like a flock of sparrows scared by a cat, each group to its own birch tree.

However, I suspect that the guards knew about these gatherings. They preferred to pretend that they didn't; it saved them the trouble of breaking them up.

Only one guard—small, quick, and overeager—was dangerous: for him, vigilance was all. He watched us, he drove us. But one time he outdid himself—pelted up to the guardhouse and announced: "There's a new sect! I saw it myself, let's go! They're all sitting in a row and singing and one is dancing in front." He led the senior duty officer over.

They were visible from a long way away, not in the park, but directly in front of the barracks: six or so old crones on a bench, singing a mournful tune. Opposite them was a tall, gray-haired woman flapping her arms high and doing squats. Every time she squatted her cropped gray locks flew upward like a fan. The guard blustered, "What's going on here! Religious gathering!"

The old women stood and bowed: "Citizen boss! Citizen boss, please let us say . . ."

But the tall gray-haired woman shouted over them, "How dare you? How dare you accuse me of any sort of religious nonsense? I've been a Party member since 1905, I've agitated against religion all my life . . . and all my life I've been doing calisthenics every morning."

"That's true," said the women. "She exercises every morning here. We just happened to sit down at the same spot, on our own."

The duty officer shot his zealous subordinate a reproachful look.

The entire camp was chuckling as news spread of the new sect.

Sometimes the prayers seemed an ancient ritual emerging out of a very deep past. One picture sticks in my mind, but is difficult to put into words; if I could, I would paint it instead.

Evening. Autumn. The birches are shedding their leaves. A lemon-yellow sunset burns through half the sky. Against that yellow light an enormous legion of crows flies, agitated and noisy. They caw as they rise, circle, and again land on the roofs around us. Black against yellow light. Against a windowless barrack wall stand the black figures of the old women. They are crossing themselves in unison, and in unison bowing from the waist, lifting their eyes to the brightly lit sky. The flock of crows circles and circles above them. The birches drop the last of their yellow leaves. Silence.

Another picture. A sunny morning, before reveille (we were allowed to relieve ourselves before the general wake-up call), I went out to the birch grove, hoping to have some time to myself. The dew was still on the grass, and a slight fog hung over the woods. Martins were flitting back and forth, preoccupied with the morning feeding of their chicks. I walked along, admiring the green shadows cast by the birches. Suddenly, from beyond one birch I heard a tearful and anxious whisper:

"Dost thou see? Dost thou see the suffering of all? Have pity, Lord. The world's suffering is without measure, but extend thy hand, and give it comfort . . . In tears I pray to thee and implore thee, for all the people, Lord!"

Trying to keep out of sight, I stepped around to see who it was. There was Annushka, standing upright, her tear-streaked face uplifted, her arms clenched to her breast. She didn't notice me, wouldn't have noticed anyone, so immersed was she in her passionate and exacting prayer for the salvation of the world.

I tiptoed away. As I was nearing the barracks, reveille sounded. Suddenly I came upon Katya Golovanova walking up the path, dressed in her best clothes.

"Katya, where are you going?"

"To our church in the birches, so that I'll have time to pray before everyone gets up."

"Annushka's out there, praying, crying . . ."

"Ah well, God be with her. I won't get in her way. I'll go someplace else."

She made a turn at the bathhouse.

7.

ISAAK FILSHTINSKY

Before he published his 1994 Gulag memoir *We March Under Guard*, Isaak Filshtinsky was better known for a different sort of writing. Born in 1918, Filshtinsky was an expert on Arab culture and literature. The author of dozens of books and articles, he was also a popular teacher at Moscow State University. Yet as a young academic he had been arrested along with many other experts in Arab and Middle Eastern cultures as a "counterrevolutionary" and potential spy. He spent six years in Kargopollag, in northern Russia, from 1949 to 1955. After his return home he developed links to the nascent Russian human rights movement, and throughout the 1960s and 1970s he was subjected to occasional searches and police interrogations. At one point, he was fired from his job.

In 1989, after the fall of the Soviet Union, he began to write an account of his camp experiences. Though not as widely known in Russia as some other memoirs, Filshtinsky's book is admired both for its high literary quality and for the author's lack of anger and resentment: his writing has a cool, distanced tone, as if it concerned the ancient Arabs whose history he knew so well, rather than his own experiences.

In the selection that follows, Filshtinsky describes a young woman, a commercial artist, whose personality is profoundly changed by her camp experience. Sensitive and frightened when he first meets her, she becomes coarse and vulgar over time. She also makes the extraordinary but not altogether uncommon transformation from prisoner to guard.

Unlike the guards in German concentration camps, Gulag guards were not considered racially superior to the prisoners, whose ethnicity they often shared. There were, for example, hundreds of thousands of Ukrainian prisoners in the camps after World War II, as well as a large number of Ukrainian guards.

Nor did the guards and prisoners inhabit distinct social spheres. Some guards had elaborate black-market dealings with prisoners. Some got drunk with prisoners. Many "cohabited" with prisoners (to use the Gulag's euphemism for sexual relations), and others employed them as unpaid servants. Many were former prisoners themselves: prisoners who were willing to collaborate, to serve as informers, and sometimes to use bribery could "graduate" to the status of guards—and some went even higher. Probably the most famous beneficiary of this system was Naftaly Frenkel, the prisoner who designed the Gulag's ration system in the

1920s, but there were others—among them, clearly, the woman in Filshtinsky's story.

Promotion

I met her purely by accident. One fairly warm autumn morning our crew was led out but for once was not marched directly to the sawmill; instead, they halted us at the guard-house at the entrance to the women's compound. Back then some camps were still holding to their wartime and postwar routines; the ban on any contact between male and female prisoners was not yet strictly enforced. When additional bodies were needed to bolster the workforce, the camp administration was in no hurry to follow the new rules to the letter; female crews were often sent out with the men's. So a small group of women joined our brigade. The two groups mixed and moved out in a single column. The women's crew consisted almost entirely of old hands, felons. All had some acquaintances among the male prisoners and felt themselves right at home.

She was darting fearful glances from side to side, backward and forward. The grim faces, the look of men long starved for a woman, their avaricious, searching eyes, their frank and predatory scrutiny of the new arrivals, their scabrous jokes would have frightened anyone. Their dress only added to the picture: ragged footwear, mangy lop-eared fur hats worn summer and winter, years on end. Filthy padded jackets and vests with tufts of singed cotton wadding sticking out of numerous holes. Work in the forest always meant working around campfires; sparks fell onto the jackets, and the cotton stuffing could smolder for hours, leaving holes with burnt edges and umber stains bleeding into the cloth.

The crew's resident joker, a *mora*—the general camp term for a Gypsy—sensed her fear. Dark eyes flashing, he slowly wove his way through the crowd, his fur hat angled down onto his forehead so that one earflap string dangled over one eye, all the better to frighten her.

In those days I was still "quarantined," in a zone within the zone. I had arrived only ten days earlier and had not yet been issued prison garb. I was still wearing the military overcoat and officer's cap that I had worn throughout all those months at Lubianka and Lefortovo. So my appearance was noticeably different from that of the longtime prisoners; this apparently prompted the young woman to wade through the crowd and seek me out. I met her timid, frightened gaze, and moving closer, asked, "Just in?"

"Yesterday, prison detail."

"Where from ?"

"Moscow: Malaia Lubianka, then Butyrka."[1]

"Article 58?"

"Yes, 58.10, five years."

---

1. These are all Moscow prisons; Malaia (small) Lubianka was used for criminal investigations.

Our column moved out, she and I marching side by side, and the woman told me her story, a fairly common one for those days. She was twenty-six, a commercial artist, had designed some exhibits, was married, and had a child—a three-year-old son. At Butyrka the interrogator told her that shortly after her arrest her husband had filed for divorce and that her mother-in-law would be rearing the boy. She had heard nothing of the child since. She'd been arrested for saying something or other to a fellow artist, who duly informed the "proper authorities." Moreover, in 1937 her father, the manager of an "elite cafeteria,"[2] had been arrested; he was accused of attempting to poison some higher-ups, who themselves were later arrested and shot. By that time the girl too was ripe for arrest, and it was easy enough to pin the same accusations on her : "enemy of the people," "terrorist intentions." But her interrogator proved to be both sympathetic and kind, and instead charged her with "anti-Soviet agitation." A mere five years.

"My interrogator was a real savior," said my new acquaintance. "He explained that if I admitted to the conversation with my girlfriend, the terrorism charge would be dropped and I wouldn't be shot."

"Oh aren't these interrogators the kindest of men," I thought. But I couldn't bring myself to disillusion her. Once she'd landed in prison, there was no way she could have avoided a stretch in the camps.

2. A dining hall restricted to top Party members.

All the way to the work site, and against all rules, the woman clung to my arm, darting fearful glances in every direction. Fortunately, the road to the sawmill was not that long, and the guard detail more or less ignored us. Once we got to the yard, the women were separated from the men and set to work stacking sawn boards, with a single guard to keep order.

When at the end of the day the crews began to form up at the guardhouse, waiting to be escorted back to their barracks, my new friend searched me out in the crowd and grabbed my arm. The thugs around us hooted encouragement: "Hey, he just got here, and look, he's already got a babe . . ."

On that first day of work my new friend had had a graphic lesson in camp morals. Barely ten minutes passed before first one then another woman began to slip away, to emerge ten or fifteen minutes later from behind the stacks, having received her ration of male love from one or another sawmill worker. Once back with her crew, the seeker of earthly delights would share her experience with her comrades, sparing no detail, however intimate. Some of the women would venture behind the stacks a number of times because, as they put it, "When's the next time you'll get to some man's . . . ?" They complained about the sad and lonely lot of the female prisoner. My friend's account was agitated, confused.

I have to say that my own lot was hardly an easy one. Months of harsh interrogation at Lubianka and Lefortovo had taken their toll, and by the end of one day in the sorting yard (we called it the sporting yard) where from seven in the morning until six at night we were unloading six-meter [twenty-foot] long boards ("fifties" and "inchers") off a never-ending conveyor, stacking them by grade onto the sledges, I could barely put one foot in front of the other. I was hardly inclined to play the role of the gallant and fearless protector of women and the oppressed, but nonetheless during that week and a half when the women's brigade was marched with us to the sawmill, I dutifully walked there and back in close company with my lady, and patiently listened to tales from her former life: the childhood that by her lights had been absolutely wonderful, the husband who had abandoned her, the child she had left behind, her life among the women convicts, her sufferings amid the cynicism and vice that surrounded her.

Prisons and camps threw people together into a cell or a compound and just as abruptly, at the whim of the interrogators and the administration, tore them apart. Cellmates, campmates often never saw each other again. So I was not at all surprised when my chance acquaintance's brigade suddenly disappeared from sawmill detail, or when the women's compound next to our lagpunkt was suddenly shut down. The women were being transferred to other units, to logging camps strung ten kilometers [six miles] along the branch line. And as usual, when someone got lost in the murky flow of camp comings and goings, we forgot that we'd ever met him. Her too.

Our joyless life in the camps dragged on, and then one day, about three years after my first meeting with my accidental friend, my brigade was being marched back from our work site to the main compound. It was a fairly warm summer day for the far North. At that time of year dusk came late; at six or seven o'clock the sun was still high and bright. Our way back led over a railroad crossing, and there at the crossing gate I saw a solitary female figure. Judging by her outward appearance, she had to be an unsupervised worker. The camp administration always had need of convicts who could work independently—for example, when logs were being hauled out of the woods and there was a one-person job to be done at a rail stop. This sort of work was assigned either to those serving light sentences or long-term prisoners who had already served most of their time. They were issued a pass that allowed them to travel unsupervised outside the zone, but only during certain hours and only along a strictly defined route. This was a privileged group. They could make a little extra money; they could buy provisions—including liquor—out in the world. If artful enough, they could have a "private life."

The woman at the crossing gate was dressed in a new prison jacket neatly tailored to her figure: it also sported a nattily upturned collar. Instead of the traditional prison-camp bonnet sewn of trouser material, she wore a beret, and shoes rather than prison-issue boots. I might not have paid much attention had it not been for one little punk in our ranks, dressed in an equally natty red shirt, who shouted out her name. The woman yelled back, and the two struck up a standard camp exchange laced with criminal argot, obscenities, and pseudo sweet-nothings. It was clear from this short conversation that the two had been lovers, but the man had been yanked back into custody for falling afoul of camp regulations. The woman swore that one day soon she would manage to get to the sawmill, where they could find a suitable hideaway for their next tryst. This exchange, amply peppered with salacious quips, testified to the woman's long and close acquaintance with the criminal world of the camps. During our short wait at the crossing the guard detail also played a lively part in the conversation, adding a little spice and edge by offering to set up a lovers' rendezvous in the cooler. They seemed to like the game, the chance to swear and blow off steam.

I took a closer look, and recognized my old friend the artist. She had gone to fat. Her face had coarsened. Her eyebrows, as Gulag fashion dictated, were plucked bare, then penciled in. Her cheeks were plastered with a thick layer of cerise and rouge. Her uneasy gaze darted back and forth, then skittered over our column. Our eyes met. She fell silent, and underneath the cerise and the rouge her cheeks reddened. She stayed absolutely silent for a few seconds, then fired another long round of abuse at her suitor, turned on her heel, and strode—almost ran—away. We moved out; she disappeared from view.

Two more years passed. By this time I was working as an inspector and was now also a trusty.[3] One of my jobs was to provide local residents with waste wood to heat

3. A trusty could not be assigned to "general work" in the forests or mines.

their houses: most of them were camp staff, some civilians, some free workers, some officers and guards on second or third tours, quartered in the village.

One day a middle-aged man showed up at the yard with a requisition for a truckload of firewood. We struck up a conversation. It turned out that he was a railroad engineer, a former convict (class of 1937) who was still banned from leaving the district in which his camp was located. He was doing work for hire, laying track that was to branch off from the Moscow-Vorkuta main line deep into Arkhangelsk Oblast as new swathes were cut and new lagpunkts established. He asked about my background, and after learning that before the war I had taken part in a few archaeological expeditions, wondered whether I knew anything about surveying. I knew less than nothing, but the temptation to change my lot in life was so strong that the longtime prisoner's reflex kicked in. Of course I knew the trade. No problem.

"We need a surveyor, someone who can travel unguarded, to plot the route. I'll try to get you reclassified," he said.

The stranger turned out to be a man of his word, and six months later I was issued a pass. But the mill bosses were reluctant to let someone who had already mastered *their* trade go off and build a railroad, and they kept me at the lumber yard. Nonetheless, at least now I was officially allowed to travel alone.

Later, after yet another screwup loading logs onto flatbeds, the yard boss, a civilian, sent me to the freight office to sort things out. I stepped through the door—and jumped. There behind an imposing desk sat (or rather, presided) my old acquaintance. To me, an old-timer by now, she looked to be dressed in the height of city fashion. At least that's how my perhaps ignorant eye took in her saucepan-shaped hat and knee-length skirt. She was berating her convict-dispatcher for sending railcars to the wrong cutting site.

"So!? What!?" she yelled. "You want to do another twenty? I can arrange that for you!"

She shot a glance at me, and seeing by my filthy jacket that I was a prisoner, barked, "And what do *you* want?"

I politely explained the reason for my visit, and when she rejected any claims or complaints from the yard, realized that our conversation was over. I was about to bow out, so to speak, and had already opened the door a crack when I felt the urge to make a little mischief. I turned and said, "You know, you and I have met! Do you remember me?"

"Of course I do. You're a goner.[4] I met you on my very first day."

"So you're a free woman now?"

"What do you think?"

"And you're married?"

"Yes."

"To whom?"

"Major L., deputy commandant in charge of discipline."

---

4. In Russian, *dokhodiaga,* a term used for prisoners who are likely to die quickly.

She spoke with a clear sense of her own dignity and the understanding that from now on she was safe and secure. Major L. was a well-known figure in the camp system. A cruel and evil man who had risen from the ranks in the 1930s, he had left a trail of victims behind him. Rumor had it that he had executed many of them himself.

We had nothing more to say to each other; I turned toward the door. But just as I was about to step across the threshold I cast a glance over my shoulder and froze in my tracks. Two wide-open, endlessly despairing eyes were fixed on me. There was a sheen about them—then again, it might have been my imagination. Another second passed, and her gaze turned calm and hard once more. Her chin shot forward, squared itself; her lips thinned to a thread. I turned and left the office without a backward glance.

8.

HAVA VOLOVICH

Hava Volovich was born in 1916. She worked as a typesetter, then as a newspaper subeditor, in a small Ukrainian town, where she watched friends and family die all around her during the famine of 1932–33. She stayed alive herself only because of the ration card she received at work. She began speaking openly and critically about the damage being done to Ukrainian peasants by the new collective farms and confiscation policies, and as a result she was arrested in 1937. She remained in the camps for sixteen years, until 1953.

After she came home, Volovich held a series of low-ranking jobs—on a pig farm, as a night watchman, as a factory stoker. Her short memoir, plainly but strongly written, appeared in 1989 along with several other women's memoirs in a much-admired anthology. Published by Vozvraschenie, an organization dedicated to the collection and preservation of Gulag memoirs, the anthology later appeared in English under the title *Till My Tale Is Told*. Even in this extraordinary collection of essays, some by famous writers, Volovich's story stands out: she, like Elena Glinka, was not afraid to touch on taboo subjects.

To my mind, the excerpt reprinted here is one of the most difficult to read in all of Gulag literature. In just a few paragraphs, Volovich narrates, with heartbreaking honesty, the story of the child born to her in the camp. This kind of story was shockingly common: there were many children born in the Gulag, as well as many children brought into the Gulag by nursing mothers. A 1949 administrative report on the condition of women recorded that of 503,000 women officially imprisoned in the Gulag, 9,300 were pregnant, and another 23,790 had small children living with them.

Because the mothers were prisoners and were supposed to be working, nurseries were created especially to care for the children. Stalin had once declared that "sons are not responsible for the crimes of their fathers," and thus the state, in theory, meant to take care of even the offspring of criminals. Gulag officials issued stern instructions from Moscow, such as one that decreed that "toys which are not spoiled by washing and boiling, made of rubber, celluloid, and bone, shall be permitted." Strict breast-feeding schedules allowed women short, twenty-minute work breaks to visit the nursery.

In practice, these places were shockingly inadequate, and many infants subjected to this kind of breast-feeding regime died. Those who made it past the first year were often deeply damaged. Yevgenia Ginzburg, who worked in one of these nurseries, recalled that many of the children had had so little human contact they could barely speak: "Inarticulate howls, mimicry, and blows were the main means of communication." She did her best to help them, as Volovich did her best to help her own child, but the powerful indifference of the camp administrators meant that many of the children suffered a terrible fate.

My Child

There was only one thing that these stockbreeders from hell could not exterminate: the sex drive. Indifferent to regulations, to the threat of the punishment cells, to hunger and humiliation alike, it lived and flourished far more openly and directly than it does in freedom.

Things that a free person might have thought about a hundred times before doing happened here as simply as they would between stray cats. No, this wasn't depravity of the kind you might expect in a brothel. This was real, "legitimate" love, with fidelity, jealousy, suffering; with the pain of parting; and with the terrible "crowning joy" of love—the birth of children.

The childbearing instinct is both beautiful and terrible. Beautiful if everything has been done to greet the arrival in the world of this new human being; terrible if this child is condemned, even before birth, to torment and suffering. But our reason was by then too blunted for us to think very carefully about the fate of our offspring.

Our need for love, tenderness, caresses was so desperate that it reached the point of insanity, of beating one's head against a wall, of suicide. And we wanted a child—the dearest and closest of all people, someone for whom we could give up our own life. I held out for a relatively long time. But I did so need and long for a hand of my own to hold, something I could lean on in those long years of solitude, oppression, and humiliation to which we were all condemned.

A number of such hands were offered, and I did not choose the best of them, by any means. But the result of my choice was an angelic little girl with golden curls. I called her Eleonora.

She was born in a remote camp barracks, not in the medical block. There were three mothers there, and we were given a tiny room to ourselves in the barracks. Bedbugs poured down like sand from the ceiling and walls; we spent the whole night brushing them off the children. During the daytime we had to go out to work and leave the infants with any old woman whom we could find who had been excused from work; these women would calmly help themselves to the food we left for the children.

I believed neither in God nor in the devil. But while I had my child, I most passionately, most violently wanted there to be a God. I wanted there to be someone who might hear my fervent prayer, born of slavery and degradation, and grant me salvation and happiness for my child, at the cost of all possible punishment and torment for myself, if need be.

Every night for a whole year, I stood at my child's cot, picking off the bedbugs and praying. I prayed that God would prolong my torment for a hundred years if it meant that I wouldn't be parted from my daughter. I prayed that I might be released with her, even if only as a beggar or a cripple. I prayed that I might be able to raise her to adulthood, even if I had to grovel at people's feet and beg for alms to do it.

But God did not answer my prayer. My baby had barely started walking—I had hardly heard her first words, the wonderful heartwarming word "Mama"—when we were dressed in rags despite the winter chill, bundled into a freight car, and transferred to the "mothers'" camp. And here my pudgy little angel with the golden curls soon turned into a pale ghost with blue shadows under her eyes and sores all over her lips.

I was put to work felling trees. On the very first day, a huge dead pine fell toward me. I saw it begin to fall, but my legs turned to water and I couldn't move. Next to me was a huge tree that had blown down in a snowstorm, and I instinctively squatted down behind its upturned roots. The pine crashed down right by me, but not even a twig touched me. I had hardly scrambled from my shelter when the brigade leader rushed up and started yelling that he didn't need sloppy workers in his brigade, and that he certainly wasn't going to answer for cretins. I let his abuse wash over me; my thoughts were far away from the pine that had so nearly killed me, and the tree felling, and the brigade leader's bad language. I could think only of my sick daughter in her cot. The next day I was transferred to the sawmill right next to the camp itself.

All that winter I sat on a frozen block of wood clutching the handle of a saw. I got a chill on the bladder and terrible lumbago, but I thanked my lucky stars for the job. I was able to take home a little bundle of firewood every day, and in return I was allowed to see my daughter outside normal visiting hours. But sometimes the guards at the gates took my firewood for themselves, causing me intense anguish.

My appearance at the time could hardly have been more miserable and wretched. To avoid getting lice (a ubiquitous delight in the camps at the time), I had shaved off my hair. Few women would have done that without being forced to. The only time I took off my padded trousers was when I was going to see my daughter.

In return for my bribes of firewood, the children's nurses, whose own children were also there in the group, would let me see my child first thing in the morning before roll call, and occasionally during the lunch break—besides, of course, at night, when I brought back the firewood.

And the things I saw there!

I saw the nurses getting the children up in the mornings. They would force them out of their cold beds with shoves and kicks. (For the sake of "cleanliness," blankets weren't tucked in around the children but were simply thrown on top of their cots.) Pushing the children with their fists and swearing at them roughly, they took off their nightclothes and washed them in ice-cold water. The babies didn't even dare cry. They made little sniffing noises like old men and let out low hoots.

This awful hooting noise would come from the cots for days at a time. Children already old enough to be sitting up or crawling would lie on their backs, their knees pressed to their stomachs, making these strange noises, like the muffled cooing of pigeons.

One nurse was responsible for each group of seventeen children. She had to sweep the ward, wash and dress the children, feed them, keep the stove going, and do all sorts of special "voluntary" shifts in the camp; but her main responsibility was keeping the ward clean. In order to cut down on her workload and allow herself a bit of free time, she would "rationalize" her jobs: that is, she would try to come up with ways in which she could reduce the amount of time she had to spend on the children. Take feeding, for instance, which I saw once.

The nurse brought a steaming bowl of porridge from the kitchen, and portioned it out into separate dishes. She grabbed the nearest baby, forced its arms back, tied them in place with a towel, and began cramming spoonful after spoonful of hot porridge down its throat, not leaving it enough time to swallow, exactly as if she were feeding a turkey chick. The fact that there was a stranger present didn't bother her: this "rationalization" had evidently been approved by someone higher up the line. No wonder there were plenty of empty beds in the infants shelter even though the birthrate in the camps was relatively high. Three hundred babies died there every year even before the war started. And how many were there during the war!

It was only their own babies whom these nurses carried around in their arms all the time, whom they fed properly, patting their bottoms tenderly; these were the only babies who lived to see freedom.

There was a doctor working in this House of Dead Babies too. Her name was Mitrikova. There was something odd and unpleasant about this woman: her movements were hasty, her speech was jerky, her eyes were always darting around. She did nothing to reduce the death rate among the infants; she cared only about the ones in the isolation ward, and even that was only for form's sake. I don't suppose the "rationalization" with the hot porridge and the loose blankets, when the temperature in the ward was only eleven or twelve degrees above freezing, was done without her knowledge either.

The few minutes that the doctor did spend in the infants' house were allocated to the groups of older children. These feeble-minded six- and seven-year-olds had somehow conformed to Darwin's law of the survival of the fittest, and they lived on despite the hot porridge, the kicks, the shoves, the washing in icy water, and the long sessions when they were left sitting on their potties tied to their chairs, a practice which meant that many children began suffering from prolapses of the large intestine.

Mitrikova did spend some time with the older children. She didn't give them any medical treatment—she had neither the wherewithal nor the skill for that—but she got them to do dances and taught them little poems and songs. Well, it was meant to look good when the time came to pack them off to an orphanage. All the children really learned in that house was the cunning and craftiness of old camp lags. They learned how to cheat and to steal, and how not to be caught doing it.

Before I had figured out what sort of person Mitrikova was, I told her how badly some of the nurses treated the children, and begged her to do something about it. She looked thunderous and promised that the guilty parties would be punished, but things remained exactly as they had been, and my little Eleonora began to fade even faster.

On some of my visits I found bruises on her little body. I shall never forget how she grabbed my neck with her tiny skinny hands and moaned, "Mama, want home!" She hadn't forgotten the bug-ridden slum where she first saw the light of day, and where she'd been with her mother all the time.

The anguish of small children is more powerful and more tragic than the anguish of adults. Knowledge comes to a child before he can fend for himself. For as long as his needs and wishes are anticipated by loving eyes and hands, he doesn't realize his own helplessness. But if those hands betray him, surrendering him to callous and cruel strangers, his horror has no limits. A child cannot grow used to things or forget them; he can only put up with them, and when that happens, anguish settles in his heart and condemns him to sickness and death.

People who find nature tidy and readily understandable may well be shocked by my view that animals are like small children, and vice versa—that is, small children are like animals. Both of them understand many things and suffer much, but since they cannot speak, they cannot beg for mercy and charity.

Little Eleonora, who was now fifteen months old, soon realized that her pleas for "home" were in vain. She stopped reaching out for me when I visited her; she would turn away in silence. On the last day of her life, when I picked her up (they allowed me to breastfeed her), she stared wide-eyed somewhere off into the distance, then started to beat her weak little fists on my face, clawing at my breast, and biting it. Then she pointed down at her bed.

In the evening, when I came back with my bundle of firewood, her cot was empty. I found her lying naked in the morgue among the corpses of the adult prisoners. She had spent one year and four months in this world, and died on March 3, 1944.

I don't know where her tiny grave is. They wouldn't let me leave the camp compound to bury her myself. By clearing the snow off the roofs of two wings of the infants' house, I earned three extra bread rations. I swapped them and my own two rations for a coffin and a small individual grave. Our brigade leader, who was allowed out without a guard, took the coffin to the cemetery and brought me back a fir twig in the shape of a cross, to stand in for a crucifix.

That is the whole story of how, in giving birth to my only child, I committed the worst crime there is.

9.

GUSTAV HERLING

When he was arrested in 1940, Gustav Herling was, at age twenty-one, already a published journalist and critic. Like Kazimierz Zarod, he was arrested in Soviet-occupied eastern Poland while trying to escape over the border. The NKVD jailed him, interrogated him, and deported him to a camp near Arkhangelsk, in the Russian far North. Finally discharged in 1942 along with other Poles, he left the country with "Anders's Army," following it through Persia and Palestine. After the war, Herling remained in Italy, not wanting to return to Soviet-dominated Poland. He made his living as an émigré writer and novelist in Naples, working for the Paris-based Polish journal *Kultura* and occasionally writing for the Italian press. He returned "home" to Poland for the first time only in 1991, after the collapse of the Communist regime.

Herling wrote his Gulag memoir *A World Apart* immediately after the war's end. In part an account of his own experiences, the book is more accurately described not as a memoir but as an exploration of the different human reactions to life in an inhuman place. It could not be published in Communist Poland, but it did appear in English in 1951, twenty years before Solzhenitsyn's writings. But although it had a preface by Bertrand Russell and was admired by Albert Camus, Herling's book never won wide renown in the West. Because its author was a Pole, it was considered too biased, too "anti-Soviet" to be taken seriously. Nevertheless, *A World Apart* did eventually appear illegally in Poland's underground press, where its impact was little short of revolutionary. Adam Michnik, one of Poland's best-known dissidents, wrote at the time of Herling's death that reading *A World Apart* at the age of fifteen had been a "shock": "All of the Communists' propaganda was reduced to nothing. I understood that every day, in school, in books, in the newspapers, they are lying to me."

The selection that follows describes an aspect of camp life which is rarely discussed elsewhere: the "house of meetings," the special barrack where prisoners were occasionally allowed to meet family members, usually their wives. Although memoirists often describe the world of the camps as separate from the "real" world, there were contacts between the two. Recent research has shown that it was possible to exchange letters more frequently than had long been assumed, at least in some camps and in some periods. Prisoners could also receive packages, and in the worst years a bar of chocolate or a hunk of lard from home might have been enough to save a life. Nevertheless, misunderstandings often arose between Gulag prisoners and their free family members–owing not least to the profound differences in the moral codes inside and outside the camp–and it is these which interest Herling the most.

The House of Meetings

Dom svidaniy, literally "the house of meetings," was the name which we gave to a newly built wing of the guardhouse, where prisoners were allowed to spend between one and three days with their relatives, who had come from all parts of Russia to the Kargopol camp for this short visit. Its topographic situation in the camp zone was to some extent symbolic: our entrance to the barrack was through the guardhouse, from the zone, and the way out was already on the other side of the barbed wire, at liberty. Thus it was easy to think that the house in which the prisoners saw their relatives for the first time after so many years was on the borderline between freedom and slavery; a prisoner, shaved, washed, and neatly dressed, having shown his pass and the official permit for the visit, walked through the partition straight into arms extended to him from liberty.

Permission for such a visit was granted only after the most complicated and trying procedure had been undergone by the prisoner as well as by his family. As far as I can remember, every prisoner was in theory allowed to have one visitor a year, but the majority of prisoners had to wait three, sometimes even five, years for it. The prisoner's part was limited: when a year had passed from the moment of his arrest, he was free to present to the Third Section[1] a written request for a visit, together with a letter from his family, which made it quite unmistakably clear that one of them wished to see him, and a certificate of his good behavior, both at work and in the barrack, from the camp authorities. This meant that a prisoner who wanted to see his mother or his wife had to work at the level of at least the second cauldron,[2] or full norm, for a year; the inhabitants of the mortuary were as a rule excluded from the privilege of a visit. The letter from the family was no mere formality. Where the connections between a prisoner and a free person were not those of blood but of marriage, the greatest pressure was put on those outside to sever all relations with the "enemy of the people," and many wives broke down under it. I read many letters in which wives wrote to their husbands in the camp, "I can't go on living like this," asking to be freed from their marriage vows. Occasionally, when the prisoner had every hope that permission for the visit would be granted, the procedure suddenly stopped dead, and only a year or two later did he learn that his relatives at liberty had thought better of it and withdrawn the original request. At other times, a prisoner who went to the house of meetings was welcomed not by extended arms, trembling with

---

1. The Third Section was the internal camp police, responsible for vetting prison visits and the collection of information from secret informers.

2. A reference to the system of giving more food to prisoners who did more work, so "at the highest level of food ration."

desire and longing, but by a look of weariness and words begging for mercy and release. Such visits confined themselves to the few hours necessary to settle the fate of the children, while the unfortunate prisoner's heart withered like a dried nut, beating helplessly within its hard shell.

The initiative in the efforts to obtain permission naturally belongs to the family at liberty. From letters which I was shown by other prisoners I gathered that the procedure is prolonged, intricate, and even dangerous. The decision does not rest with GULAG (the Central Office of Camp Administration), which is concerned only with the administration of the camps and has nothing to do with the sentences or the indictments which produced them, but nominally with the Chief Prosecutor of the USSR, and actually with the local NKVD office in the petitioner's place of domicile. A free person who is sufficiently obstinate to persist in his audaciousness, undeterred by the initial obstacles, finds himself the victim of a vicious circle from which he can seldom escape. Only a person with an absolutely blameless political past, one who can prove that he is immune from the germ of counter-revolution, can obtain the precious permission. Now in Russia no one would dare enter a hearing of interrogation even with a totally clear conscience; in this case, too, the certificate of political health is demanded by officials who are the only ones with the authority to give it. Apart from this evident contradiction, we find another, even more fantastic. The presence in one's family of an enemy of the people is in itself sufficient proof of contamination, for someone who has lived with him during many years cannot be free from the plague of counter-revolution.

The NKVD treat political offenses as a contagious disease. Thus when a petitioner arrives at the NKVD office for a certificate of health, that in itself is evidence of his probable infection. But let us suppose that the political blood tests have not shown the presence of infection in the organism, and the petitioner has been vaccinated and remains in quarantine for an indefinite time. If all goes well, he then receives permission for a direct, three-day contact with the sick man, whose very existence seemed at the interrogation to be dangerous even at a distance of several thousand miles. The cruel, discouraging paradox of this situation is that during the hearings at the NKVD the petitioner must do everything to convince the interrogator that he has broken all relations with the prisoner and eradicated all emotional ties with him. And back comes the obvious question: in that case, why should he be willing to undertake a distant and expensive journey in order to see the prisoner? There is no way out of this conundrum. No obstacle is put in the way of wives who ask for a visit to the camp in order to end their marriages, thus freeing themselves from the nightmare of a life in half-slavery, in an atmosphere of constant suspicion, and with the brand of shared responsibility for the crimes of others. Others either give it up or else take the final, desperate step— a journey to Moscow to obtain the permission through special influence there. Even if they do somehow succeed by this method, they will have to face the vengefulness of the local NKVD, whom they have slighted to achieve their object, when they return from the camp to their native town. It is easy to guess how many are brave enough to risk asking for permission under these circumstances.

It is natural to ask why these monstrous difficulties and obstacles are put in the way of a visit, since the contingent of workers has already been supplied to the camps, and the costs of the journey there are covered by the visitor himself. I can only suggest three possible conjectures, of which one at least is accurate. Either the NKVD sincerely believes in its mission of safeguarding the Soviet citizen's political health; or it attempts as far as possible to conceal from free people the conditions of work in forced labor camps, and to induce them by indirect pressure to break off all relations with their imprisoned relatives; or in this way it is putting power into the hands of camp authorities, which during whole years can squeeze from prisoners the remnants of their strength and health, deluding them with the hope of an imminent visit.

When the relative, usually the prisoner's wife or mother, at last finds herself in the Third Section office of the particular camp, she must sign a declaration promising not to disclose by even one word, after her return home, what she has seen of the camp through the barbed wire; the privileged prisoner signs a similar declaration, undertaking—this time under pain of heavy punishment, even of death—not to mention in conversation his and his fellow-prisoners' life and conditions in the camp. One can imagine how difficult this regulation makes any direct or intimate contact between two people who, after many years of separation, meet for the

first time in these unusual surroundings; what is left of a
relationship between two people if an exchange of mutual
experiences is excluded from it? The prisoner is forbidden to
say, and the visitor forbidden to ask, what he has gone
through since the day of his arrest. If he has changed beyond
recognition, if he has become painfully thin, if his hair has
turned gray and he has aged prematurely, if he looks like a
walking skeleton, he is allowed only to remark casually that
"he hasn't been feeling too well, for the climate of this part
of Russia does not suit him." Having thrown a cloak of silence over what may be the most important period of his
life, the regulations push him back to an already distant and
dimly remembered past, when he was at liberty and an entirely different man, when he felt and thought differently; he
is in the unbearable situation of a man who should be free to
speak, to shout even, and who is allowed only to listen. I
have no idea whether all prisoners keep the promise given
before the meeting, but, taking into consideration the high
price which they would have to pay for breaking it, it may
be supposed that they do. It is true that the closeness of the
visiting relative may be some guarantee of discretion, but
who is to say whether the tiny room, in which the two live
together during the whole visit, is not supplied with an
eavesdropping microphone, or whether a Third Section official is not listening on the other side of the partition? I only
know that I often heard sobbing as I passed by the house of
meetings, and I believe that this helpless, spasmodic weeping
relieves their tension and expresses for the wretched human
tatters, now dressed in clean prison clothing, all that they

may not say in words. I think, too, that this is one of the advantages of a visit, for a prisoner seldom dares to cry in front of his companions, and the nightly sobbing in their sleep in the barrack proved to me that it could bring great relief. In the emptiness which sealed lips create between the two people in the house of meetings, they advance cautiously like lovers who, having lost their sight during long years of separation, reassure themselves of each other's tangible existence with tentative caresses until, at the moment when they have finally learned to communicate in the new language of their feelings, they must part again. That is why prisoners after their return from the house of meetings were lost in thought, disillusioned, and even more depressed than before the longed-for visit.

Victor Kravchenko, in *I Chose Freedom*,[3] tells the story of a woman who, after many attempts and in return for a promise of cooperation with the NKVD, was finally given permission to visit her husband in a camp in the Urals. Into the small room at the guardhouse shuffled an old man in filthy rags, and it was only with difficulty and after several moments that the young woman recognized her husband. It is more than likely that he had aged and changed, but I cannot believe that he was in rags. I cannot, of course, make a categorical statement about conditions in the Ural camps, and I can only answer for what I myself saw, heard, or lived

---

3. *I Chose Freedom*, a memoir by Victor Kravchenko (1905–66), had an enormous impact on the postwar European left, causing many to abandon communism.

through in a camp near the White Sea. Nevertheless, I believe that all forced-labor camps throughout Soviet Russia, though they differ greatly in various respects, had a common aim, possibly imposed upon them from above: they strive at all costs to maintain, before free Soviet citizens, the appearance of normal industrial enterprises which differ from other sections of the general industrial plan only by their employment of prisoners instead of ordinary workers, prisoners who are quite understandably paid slightly less and treated slightly worse than if they were working of their own free will. It is impossible to disguise the physical condition of prisoners from their visiting relatives, but it is still possible to conceal, at least partly, the conditions in which they live. In Yercevo, on the day before the visit, the prisoner was made to go to the bathhouse and to the barber; he gave up his rags in the store of old clothing and received—only for the three days of the visit—a clean linen shirt, clean underwear, new wadded trousers and jerkin, a cap with earflaps in good condition, and boots of the first quality; from this last condition were exempt only prisoners who had managed to preserve, for just such an occasion, the suit which they had worn at the time of their original arrest, or to acquire one, usually in a dishonest way, while serving their sentence. As if this were not enough, the prisoner was issued with bread and soup tickets for three days in advance; he usually ate all the bread by himself there and then, to eat his fill just once, and the soup tickets he distributed among his friends, relying on the food which would be brought by the visitor.

When the visit was over, the prisoner had to submit all that he had received from his relatives to an inspection at the guardhouse; then he went straight to the clothing store to shed his disguise and take up his true skin once more. These regulations were always very strictly enforced, though even here there were glaring contradictions which could at once destroy the whole effect of this comedy staged for the benefit of free citizens of the Soviet Union. On the first morning of a visit the relative could, by raising the curtain in the room, catch a glimpse of the brigades marching out from the guardhouse to work beyond the zone and see the dirty, scrofulous shadows wrapped in torn rags held together with string, gripping their empty mess cans and swooning from cold, hunger, and exhaustion; only an imbecile could have believed that the scrubbed, neat man who had been brought to the house of meetings the day before in clean underwear and new clothes had avoided the fate of the others. This revolting masquerade was sometimes comic despite its tragic implication, and a prisoner in his holiday outfit was greeted by jeers from the others in the barrack. I thought that if someone would fold the hands of these living dead, dressed in their tidy suits, over their chests, and force a holy picture and a candle between their stiffened fingers, they could be laid out in oak coffins, ready for their last journey. Needless to say, the prisoners who were forced to take part in this exhibition felt awkward in their disguise, as if ashamed and humiliated by the thought that they were being made use of as a screen to hide the camp's true face for three days.

The house itself, seen from the road which led to the camp from the village, made a pleasant impression. It was built of rough pine beams, the gaps filled in with oakum; the roof was laid with good tiling; and fortunately the walls were not plastered. We all had occasion to curse the plaster with which the barrack walls in the camp were covered: water from melted snowdrifts, and urine made by prisoners against the barracks at night, disfigured the white walls with yellow-gray stains, which looked from a distance like the unhealthy pimples of acne on a pale, anemic face. During the summer thaw the thin plaster peeled off the walls, and then we walked through the zone without looking to right or left—the holes corroded in the brittle crust of whitewash by the climatic scurvy seemed to remind us that the same process was corrupting our bodies. If only because of the contrast, it was pleasant to rest our weary eyes by gazing at the house of meetings, and not without cause (though its appearance was not the only reason) was it known as "the health resort." The door outside the zone, which could be used only by the free visitors, was reached by a few solid wooden steps; cotton curtains hung in the windows, and long windowboxes planted with flowers stood on the windowsills. Every room was furnished with two neatly made beds, a large table, two benches, a basin and a water jug, a clothes cupboard, and an iron stove; there was even a lampshade over the electric lightbulb. What more could a prisoner, who had lived for years on a common bunk in a dirty barrack, desire of this model petit bourgeois dwelling? Our dreams of life at liberty were based on that room.

Every prisoner was given a separate room, but the prison rules broke that intimacy brutally by making clear distinctions between the privileges of free men and the obligations of prisoners serving a sentence of forced labor. The visiting relative was at liberty to leave the house at any time of the day and night to go to the village, but always alone: the prisoner had to remain in the same room during the whole visit, or else, if he so wished, he could return to the zone for a few minutes after first being searched at the guardhouse. In exceptional cases the permission was burdened by an additional provision, which confined the visit to the daytime: the prisoner returned to his barrack in the evening and came back to the house of meetings at dawn (I could never think of a reason for this cruelty; some prisoners believed that it was a form of deliberate persecution, but this was not confirmed by general practice). In the mornings, when the brigades passed the house of meetings on their way to work, the curtains in its windows were usually drawn slightly aside, and we saw our fellow prisoners inside with strange, free faces. We usually slowed down and dragged our legs in a slightly exaggerated manner, as if to show the "people from over there" to what life behind barbed wire had brought us. We were allowed to give no other sign of recognition, just as we were forbidden to wave to passengers on passing trains as we passed by the railway tracks (the guards had strict orders to drive their brigades into the forest, away from the railway tracks, whenever they heard the sound of an approaching train). The prisoners in the windows of the house of meetings frequently smiled at us and sometimes greeted us by fondly embracing their visitor, as if in this simple and touching way they wanted to remind us that they were human, with well-dressed relatives, free to touch intimately those "from the other side." But more often tears stood in their faded eyes, and painful spasms passed through the haggard faces; perhaps it was our own wretchedness which thus moved those more fortunate prisoners who saw us through the window of a warm, clean room, or perhaps it was only the thought that tomorrow or the day after they themselves would be back in the brigades, hungry and cold, marching off for another twelve hours in the forest.

The situation of those free women who, after surmounting countless obstacles, have at last succeeded in reaching the camp for a visit, is no more enviable. They feel the boundless suffering of the prisoner without fully understanding it or being in any way able to help; the long years of separation have killed much of their feeling for their husbands, and they come to the camp only to warm them, during three short days, with the embers of their love—the flame could not be rekindled from the spark hidden in the warm heart of ashes. The camp, distant and barred off from the visitor, yet casts its shadowy menace on them. They are not prisoners, but they are related to those enemies of the people. Perhaps they would more willingly agree to accept the prisoner's burden of hatred and suffering than to suffer in silence the humiliating and equivocal situation of borderland inhabitants. The camp officials treat them politely and correctly, but at the same time with almost undisguised reserve and contempt. How can they show respect to the wife or the mother of a wretch who begs for a spoonful of soup, rummages in the rubbish heaps, and has long since lost any feeling of his own human dignity? In Yercevo village, where every new face left no doubt as to its owner's purpose in the town, visitors to the camp were cautiously avoided. One prisoner told me that when his daughter visited him in the camp she met an old friend, now the wife of one of the camp officials, in the village. They greeted each other with pleasure, but after a while the official's wife drew back anxiously. "What a coincidence, meeting you here! But what are you doing in Yercevo?" "Oh," answered the girl, "I've come to visit my father. You can imagine how unhappy we are!" and added, "Of course, he isn't at all guilty," as if hoping that after breaking the ice she would succeed in obtaining some consideration for her father in the camp. But the other woman left her coldly, saying, "Good. You should write a complaint to Moscow, they will look into it there."

Although, or perhaps because, these visits were so rare and so difficult to obtain, they played a large part in the life of the camp. I became convinced while I was still in prison that if a man has no clear end in life—and the ending of his sentence and his final release were too distant and uncertain to be seriously taken into account—he must at least have something to anticipate. Letters were so rare, and their language so commonplace and restricted, that they had no attraction as an object of expectation; only the visits were left to the prisoners. They waited for them with anxiety and joyful tension, and often reckoned the time of their sentences or their lives by those short moments of happiness, or even its very anticipation. Those who still had not been informed of a definite date for their visits lived on hope; they possessed something to occupy them, and perhaps even more, a quiet passion which saved them from utter despair, from the fatal consciousness of their aimless existence. They fed their hope artificially, wrote requests and applications to Moscow, bore the heaviest work manfully like pioneers building their own future; in the evenings they talked to their more fortunate comrades, repeatedly asking what ways there were of hastening that wonderful event; on rest days they stood outside the house of meetings, as if to make sure that their rooms were reserved and only awaiting the arrival of the guests, quarreled among themselves in advance over the choice of rooms, and endlessly cleaned and darned their best clothes. Lonely prisoners and foreigners were naturally in the worst position, but even they were able to draw some benefit from the visits, sharing as they did in the happiness and expectation of others, or recognizing them to be their only source of information about life outside, at liberty.

Men isolated forcibly, or even voluntarily, from the rest of the world, idealize everything that occurs beyond the frontiers of their solitude. It was touching to hear prisoners before the expected visit recalling the liberty whose mere taste they were about to enjoy. It seemed that never before in their lives had they experienced either important events or bitter disappointments. Freedom for them was the one blessed irreplaceable. At liberty one slept, ate, and worked differently; there the sun was brighter, the snow whiter, and the frost less painful. "Remember? Remember?"—excited voices whispered on the bunks. "I remember, at liberty, I was stupid and wouldn't eat brown bread." And another would take up: "I wasn't satisfied with Kursk, I wanted Moscow. Just wait till my wife comes, I'll tell her what I think of Kursk now, just wait till I tell her . . ." These conversations sometimes dragged on till late into the night, but they were never heard on bunks where a prisoner who had recently returned from a visit lay. The illusion had come face to face with the reality, and the illusion always suffered. Whatever the reasons for their disappointment—whether the freedom, realized for three days, had not lived up to its idealized expectation, whether it was too short, or whether, fading away like an interrupted dream, it had left only fresh emptiness in which they had nothing to wait for—the prisoners were invariably silent and irritable after visits, to say nothing of those whose visits had been transformed into a tragic formality of separation and divorce. Krestynski, a joiner from the 48th Brigade, twice attempted to hang himself after an interview with his wife, who had asked him for a divorce and for his agreement to place their children in a municipal nursery. I came to the conclusion that if hope can often be the only meaning left in life, then its realization may sometimes be an unbearable torment.

Younger prisoners suffered additional and, at least as far as their neighbors on the bunk were concerned, by no means intimate sexual anxieties before visits from their wives. Years of heavy labor and hunger had undermined their virility, and now, before an intimate meeting with an

almost strange woman, they felt, besides nervous excitement, helpless anger and despair. Several times I did hear
men boasting of their prowess after a visit, but usually these
matters were a cause for shame, and respected in silence by
all prisoners. Even the *urkas*[4] murmured indignantly whenever a guard who during his night duty at the guardhouse
had relieved his boredom by listening through the thin partition to the sounds of love from the other side, derisively
shared his observations with other prisoners in the brigade.
Unbridled sexual depravity was the rule in the zone, where
women were treated like prostitutes and love like a visit to
the latrine, and where pregnant girls from the maternity hut
were greeted with coarse jokes. Yet the house of meetings,
in this pool of filth, degradation, and cynicism, had become
the only haven of whatever emotional life memory had
brought into the camp from liberty. I remember our joy when
one of the prisoners received a letter telling him of the birth
of a child conceived during a visit from his wife. If that child
could have been given to us, we would have looked upon it
as our common child, we would have fed it, going hungry
ourselves, and passed it from hand to hand, even though
there were plenty of brats conceived on a barrack bunk.
That, for us, was the most important difference: they had
been conceived on a barrack bunk in the zone, not in the
house of meetings with a free woman and on clean sheets . . .
In that way only did life allow us, dead and forgotten men,

4. Camp slang for habitual criminals.

to feel a slight bond with freedom despite our incarceration in that earthly tomb.

What else can I say about our house of meetings? Perhaps only that as a foreigner I never expected to see anyone there, and possibly that is why my observations about the behavior of my fellow prisoners, whose joys and disappointments I shared only involuntarily, are so objective and so indifferent even to pain.

10.

LEV KOPELEV

Born in 1912, Lev Kopelev came of age as an idealistic Communist. As a working journalist, he witnessed the confiscation of grain from the Ukrainian peasants in 1931, the policy which led to the onset of a mass famine. Nevertheless, he retained his faith in the ultimate goodness of the system, even rising to become a major in the Red Army's notorious Political Department, the institution that maintained ideological control over the soldiers. Only at the end of the war, horrified by the wanton rapes and murders he had witnessed during the Soviet invasion of East Prussia, did Kopelev begin to become disillusioned. He wrote a letter to his superiors condemning the Red Army's behavior. For this he was arrested in 1945. Kopelev served a nine-year sentence, partly in Unzhlag, a camp in the Volga region, where he worked in a camp hospital, and partly in a Moscow *sharashka* (prison for scientists). Inmates in sharaskas were better housed and fed, and were allowed to conduct scientific experiments. Some of Russia's most

distinguished engineers spent time in them, as did Solzhenitsyn, who met Kopelev in a sharashka and later used him as
the basis for a character in his novel *The First Circle*. Kopelev was rehabilitated in 1954 and returned to Moscow,
where he became a literary critic and writer. In that capacity,
he was able to help Solzhenitsyn publish his novel *A Day in
the Life of Ivan Denisovich*, the only true piece of Gulag
literature to appear in the years before perestroika. But
over time Kopelev's disillusion grew, and he was drawn, like
many former Gulag prisoners, to the human rights movement. He broke with the Party following the Soviet invasion
of Czechoslovakia in 1968, and in 1980 the Soviet Union
revoked his citizenship. He spent the rest of his life in exile
in Germany.

Kopelev published many books, among them his memoir *To Be Preserved Forever*, whose title echoes the phrase
stamped on prisoners' files. Kopelev wrote the book in the
early 1970s and had it smuggled out of the Soviet Union
and published abroad in 1975. The selection reprinted here
describes an episode that illustrates the deep ambiguities
always present in camp life, as well as the camp system's
strange morality. The subject is informers—people who collaborated with camp authorities and secretly reported on
their fellow prisoners—and the kinds of retaliation that
other inmates frequently deployed against them. Informers
were an intrinsic part of the Soviet system in many other
spheres, of course, but in camps they were often spoken of,
and dealt with, in a far more open way than they could be
in the "free" Soviet Union. At the time of this incident Ko-

pelev was studying to be a *feldsher*, a nurse, a job coveted
by many of the educated prisoners.

Informers

In prison we used to be afraid of informers and talked
about them in whispers. Here in the camp we spoke of them
out loud. The lowest of all the minions of the mighty state,
as helpless and humiliated as the rest of us, and often as
falsely accused and as unfairly sentenced, they were nevertheless the indispensable cogs of the cruel punitive machine.
They served for the sake of the little handouts the machine
threw their way, and they served out of fear.

An informer talking: "I'll tell you, as one frontliner to
another, even in a camp a man can make out. A camp has its
own laws. All you have to do is follow them."

I listen. I like to find out what made them sink so low.

"They'll tell you I'm a stool pigeon, and maybe you'll
think that I'm a rat, that there's nothing I wouldn't stoop to.
Well, don't you believe it.

"True, I have some business with the Oper"[1]—you know,
the one they call the godfather. Of course I do—I'm a patriot,

---

1. The Operational Representative of the secret police, who also
organized the network of prisoner informers. All camps had at least one
Oper. Prisoners referred to them by many slang names, including *koum*,
"godfather."

I used to belong to the Komsomol. And who is he? The representative of the Cheka, and this camp is full of enemies of the people. Of course, there's also the other kind, like you and me. I can tell about people. I was educated. And life taught me plenty. I've been in the Crimea, in Rome, in Germany, and in France. As a prisoner of the Germans, of course. *Boche cochon, Russe très bien. Vive la France, vive la Russie!*[2] You understand? Of course you do. You're educated, too—I could tell about you at once. If the Oper asks me about you, I'll say, 'He's one of us, law-abiding, a patriot.'"

Then, without stopping for breath, without a change of tone: "You have any buddies? Only one? Which one? Oh. What does he do? Was he in the Party? Was he taken prisoner? Oh. And you believe him? I'll tell you, as one frontliner to another, don't believe what you hear. One buddy—that's all right. But if anyone else tries to get friendly, you come to me—I'll tell you what he's after. The cook, for instance. He's a stoolie—hates everyone like you who's here under Article 58. Be careful of him.

"Have some tobacco—first-class quality, this. You want to go to the bathhouse before you turn in—come to me. You want some underclothes, some soap—"

He goes on and on, endlessly. Why the confession? Some particularly subtle game? Or some human need to reveal himself or to play the big shot?

---

2. "Kraut, pig, Russian very good. Long live France, long live Russia!"

Another informer: "Ah, you've got some books. I can see you're a cultured man. I also love books. Gorky, Kuprin, Ehrenburg . . . And do you get newspapers, too? What do you think of this Churchill? He was our ally, our buddy, and now, did you see what he said about us?"

On another day, mysteriously: "I want to talk to you privately. I know you're a good guy, but . . . Just by chance I found out—somebody squealed—that you and this nurse are, as they say . . . Well, I want to tell you as a friend: to-night, be careful. There's going to be an inspection. I found out by accident. I hope that as a cultured man, you won't tell anyone I told you . . ."

Uncle Nechipor and young Iosip were Baptists. The older man had been nursed back to relative health, but they kept him on in our ward while putting him to work tending the heating system. Iosip, recovering from an operation for a chronic ear infection, was pale and thin and the youngest in our fourteen-man ward. When anyone spoke to him, he smiled sweetly. "As the Lord wills," he would say, and "God bless you."

Nechipor, polite and companionable, would tell us of miracles performed through faith—of the fatally ill cured by the power of prayer, of bums, thieves, and errant hus-bands reformed by Holy Scripture. But in the evenings he would often take Iosip out into the corridor so they would not hear our "worldly" conversations. Sometimes we would hear them singing softly in harmony.

The feast is spread, the guests rejoice,
And Jesus calls you to his side.
Why do you not hear his voice?
Why does your timid spirit hide?

My new buddy, Seriozha, was a raw kid sentenced to ten years for having contemplated deserting to the Germans when his frontline unit was surrounded in the summer of '42—even though the plan, put to him by others, had never been carried out. He would receive parcels from his working-class family in Moscow; my parcels kept arriving every two weeks or so; and both of us would share our bounty with the others in the ward—most particularly with poor, sick, uncomplaining Iosip.

One day Nechipor received a parcel of cereal, cheese, pork fat, and homegrown tobacco (the last to be realized into cash, since, as a Baptist, he did not smoke). Nechipor cooked some gruel, thickened it with lard, and brought in four platefuls—for Seriozha, me, and two others in our ward.

As we ate, Iosip looked on sadly, meekly, unable to avert his eyes. We went into the kitchen and said, "Uncle Nechipor, thank you, but aren't you forgetting Iosip? He is hungrier than we are."

"You gave me to eat," Nechipor replied in his cheerful, self-assured way, "and now I am giving you to eat. As the Bible says, 'Give, and it shall be given unto you. Repay good with good.' I love Brother Iosip with my soul, but I love all men and I do not have enough to give to all."

"But Iosip needs it more than anyone. He's so thin he's practically transparent!"

"That is the cross he has been given to bear. Whom the Lord loves he burdens with tests. Brother Iosip bears his cross humbly and gains virtue in the sight of God."

This was too much for Seriozha. "You—you kulak, you lousy bloodsucker!" He let loose a string of blasphemous oaths.

Nechipor turned away. After that he held himself at a distance and avoided looking at us. If we happened to meet in the morning, he would say hello with a soft, sad voice. He forgave his enemies.

The director of our hospital was a young woman who had graduated as surgeon before the war and had served at the front, with the rank of captain. She now wore the uniform of the Ministry of Internal Affairs,[3] but she retained some of the decisiveness and informality of frontline doctors and treated the two men under her as colleagues, though both were convicts, in the camp since 1938. One was Boris Liebenson (Uncle Boria), who was in charge of our section. The other was Nikolai Teliants, chief surgeon for the entire hospital.

Teliants was an Armenian, a son of the craggy Caucasus, who took great pride in the history of his ancient, brave, and wise people. He had been deputy people's commissar for

---

3. The ministry in charge of the Gulag.

public health in the Tajik Soviet Socialist Republic and had been arrested and tried together with the entire Tajik government. He never talked about that but liked to discuss philosophy, literature, and history. He was demanding and hot-tempered—even the hospital director was a little afraid of his sharp tongue—and he made no secret of his hatred of informers.

As winter wore into spring and I began to study to become a male nurse while working in the boot shop, Teliants and the other doctors warned me that one of our orderlies, Stepan, was an informer. Stepan was another of those unfortunates who had been sentenced for falling prisoner to the Germans. Silent, slack-jawed, and melancholy, he always seemed to be present when any of us were talking about anything out of the ordinary.

We became conscious of it only when we found out that he was an informer. Pan Leon, a former fur dresser from Belorussia, whose case, like mine, was still before the courts, would challenge him loudly. "Why are you hanging around us, Stepan? Is there something you want? What is it? Tell us; don't be shy."

Stepan would grin uncomfortably. "I'm just . . . I'm only . . ." He would flush and perspire. "What's the matter; can't I stand where I want to? What are you afraid of—that I'll wear a hole in the floor?"

Some of the others in our company made their feelings even plainer. One of them, a young village tough named Vasia, once "accidentally" dug his elbow into Stepan's midriff so forcefully that Stepan gasped for breath. Another time, seeing Stepan standing in the doorway, he charged out to the toilet, knocking Stepan violently aside. "Out of the way, you lump of carrion—can't you see I'm in a hurry?"

Vasia liked to tell stories in Stepan's presence of how they had disposed of "Judas-informers" in his former prison barracks. "We took this stool pigeon by the arms and legs and swung him up—high, high. Then we brought him down on the floor, right on his ass. Again, and again, and again. You couldn't see any marks on him. But the next day he was spitting blood. A week later he was dead. His kidneys were gone."

Stepan listened with seeming unconcern, a drop collecting at the end of his nose.

Stepan's assignment from the Oper was no sinecure. He had to haul sacks of bread, buckets of balanda,[4] and other supplies from the distributing center to our kitchen, where the food was warmed before serving; he had to serve the meals, keep the place clean, lead those who could walk to the bathhouse, help carry the bedridden on stretchers to the X-ray room, get the linen to the laundry and back, and do a variety of other odd jobs. Trying to ingratiate himself with us, he would get us additional food whenever he could. "Got this little extra for our gang," he would confide in a stage whisper. "Pull is stronger than Council of People's Commisars."

He was at his most zealous when the blood was handed out. Sometimes, in addition to the usual gruel for dinner, we

4. Camp slang for prison soup.

were given rations of coagulated blood, said to be very
good for pellagra. Many of us refused to touch it, hungry as
we were; it stank too much of carrion. So a lot of it was
left over. Bringing in a trayful of dark-brown clots, Stepan
would sing out: "If you're delicate, light up; if you're a
blood drinker, set to! Lots for everyone!" He became lively
and talkative, feeling more than ever the benefactor.

Pan Leon and Vasia were in awe of medicine; besides,
Pan Leon never gave and never turned down anything and
Vasia never got food parcels. So, unlike Seriozha and me,
they gobbled up the dried blood and took a kindlier view of
Stepan.

Aunt Dusia, our housekeeper, was a small, prematurely
withered woman with big gray youngish eyes smiling out of
a wrinkled face. Her voice was hurried, eager, with a musical lilt. Never did a bitter or unseemly word come from her
mouth: a reproachful "Now, dearie," or a resigned "*Ekh*,
you cabbage head," was the closest I heard her come to anger. She had spent more years in labor camps than anyone
else I had met—since 1932. I liked to listen to her peasant
speech.

. . .

Aunt Dusia's room was next to the kitchen. It was in the
kitchen, where I could read and smoke after lights out in
the wards, and which also served as the duty room for the
night nurse, that my liaison with the nurse Edith began.

Edith, who was from one of the ethnic-German areas, was serving the last two years of a ten-year sentence.

In April of that year Aunt Dusia invited us to a secret observance of Easter. One of the inmates tending the stoves was a priest, two of the laundresses were nuns, one of the cooks was an expert in religious services, and the four of them, together with Aunt Dusia, had made one of the women's barracks into an improvised chapel, greasing palms wherever necessary to keep it quiet.

Seriozha was invited as well.

"So what if you are unbelievers?" Aunt Dusia said. "You and Seriozha stand up for people, and whoever stands up for people stands up for God. Your Nechipor, the Baptist, is always talking about God, and I don't believe him. But you and Seriozha, and your Edith, you are people with soul. I see right into you, and what I see is good, and I pray for you as for one of my own."

The service was held in the evening. The beds were placed alongside the walls. There was a fragrant smell of incense. A little table covered by a blanket was the altar. Several homemade candles cast their glow on an icon. The priest, wearing vestments made of sheets, held up an iron cross.

The candles flickered in the dark. We could hardly see the faces of the others in the room, but I felt sure that we were not the only unbelievers present. The priest chanted the service in an old man's quaver. Several women in white kerchiefs joined in softly, their voices ardent and pure.

A choir gave harmonious responses, softly, softly, in order not to be heard outside.

There, outside, ten steps from the barracks walls, was the barbed wire, with its watchtowers, its sentries in sheep-skin coats; and, further on, the houses of the guards and the camp officials; and beyond them, all around us, the dense and ancient forest; and beyond the forest, the west, the Volga, and a string of villages, gray and hungry; and finally, hun-dreds of kilometers away, Moscow. The ruby stars in the Kremlin towers. An old, peeling house. A narrow room, where my daughters were asleep. And beyond Moscow, toward the west, a trail of ruins, ashes, and freshly dug graves . . .

The next day, Easter Sunday, some of us were invited to Aunt Dusia's room. Each of us had tried to contribute something, and she had prepared a festive spread. There were hard-boiled eggs, painted according to Easter custom, and meat and baked potatoes; there were American canned beef and sausage, and biscuits and sweets—the yield of parcels from home. The doctors had contributed some alcohol, which Aunt Dusia had mixed with a bottle of liquid vitamins for color and taste. She had even managed to bake a kulich[5] and to adorn it with colored paper flowers. We exchanged the traditional Easter toast—"Christ is risen!" "Truly risen!"— and Aunt Dusia took two plates of food and two glasses of

5. Traditional Russian Easter bread.

the improvised vodka to Uncle Boria and Dr. Teliants, who lived in the doctors' house.

Aunt Dusia also insisted that we invite the informer Stepan.

"Dearie," she argued, "with his poor, lost, dark, sinful soul, where will he find a ray of light if we don't show it to him? Let him see that even here, in prison, the light of Christ still shines and there is pity even for such as he. We didn't tell him about the church service, because others would be held responsible if it became known. We invited only those we could be sure of. But here in my little room I am mistress. Around this little table we are all equal, believers and unbelievers, and for all of us this is a bright holiday, and there is only good here.

"And there is another reason. Oh, dearie, don't think I haven't learned. I'm a crafty one, I am. Just think— everybody who drops in for a bite and a drink—don't you think Stepan will smell the alcohol on their breath? You'll take a little food to your friends in your ward—don't you think he'll ask: from where? His eyes, his ears, his nose are always on the job, and so he'll have to squeal on us. But if we invite him and treat him and exchange toasts with him, in Christ's holy name—for Jesus taught us to love and pity our enemies—he will see things differently, and he will not be able to repay good with evil."

Aunt Dusia did as she proposed. She called Stepan, and poured a drink for him, and exchanged the Easter toast with him. And Stepan drank and ate and beamed. "Thank you—thank you." He even winked, as though to say that he understood and that there was no need to worry.

We were all in a tender mood and smiled and said kind things to each other. Someone made a speech about this being a holiday not only for Christians but for all men of goodwill. I argued compellingly that a good Christian and a good Communist not only shouldn't, but couldn't, be enemies.

Two days later, Aunt Dusia, her face stained with tears, told us that Stepan had squealed. She had her own intelligence network and usually knew what was going on. She had learned that Stepan had reported the reception to the Oper. The Oper wanted to conduct an investigation, but Uncle Boria and Dr. Teliants opposed the idea, and the hospital director sided with her convict-doctors. Instead, as a compromise measure, Aunt Dusia was to be transferred to a harder post in a sewing shop.

There were more tears, particularly among the younger nurses, the day she left. Stepan was replaced as orderly and transferred to an adjoining barracks. If we ran into him after that, we pretended not to see him; when he spoke, we pretended not to hear. For us, he ceased to exist. But Seriozha swore he'd kill him; it was only a question of finding a way.

I told the whole story to Dr. Teliants.

"Don't do anything," he said. "Tell your friend to lay off. Leave it to me."

About a week later, I reminded him of his words.

"I haven't forgotten."

One evening in May, I was having dinner in the kitchen with Edith when an orderly came in. "The doctor wants you to play chess with him."

I went to his room. Dr. Teliants sat before a chessboard.

"Some of our convalescents are well enough to go back to work. There's a batch of them leaving for Post No. 18 tonight. I've added that snake of yours to the list. Have the telephone operator call Post No. 18 and give them his name. Just a hint will be enough."

Dr. Teliants spoke absently, as though concentrating on the chess problem before him. Then he looked up. "Have a seat. We'll play a game. You will also observe a little scene. Only no commentaries, if you please."

Post No. 18 was located in the thick of a swampy forest and had one of the heaviest labor regimes in the whole camp. Where you were sent after you regained your health depended partly on luck, partly on the wishes of the hospital authorities, who could hold up your transfer until there was a transport for one of the softer work posts or who could wait until a transport for one of the hard-labor posts came by. Those authorized to decide were the hospital director, her deputy, and the chief surgeon, Dr. Teliants. On this particular day the director and her deputy were both away on a trip to Gorky, and Dr. Teliants was in charge.

We had hardly made the opening moves when there was a knock on the door. A woman secretary entered. "Doctor, here's this list. Here's a zek[6] named—" Noticing me, she faltered. "Well, the Operational Representative says this zek shouldn't be sent with the others."

"Which zek?" Dr. Teliants looked at her list. "Ah, that one. He has recovered. Fully. I ordered him sent off. So there's no reason for the citizen Operational Representative to be concerned. Understood?"

"Understood . . ."

The secretary lingered, disconcerted. She was a free citizen, attached to the camp administration; he was an inmate. But he was the "wild doctor," a legend to the whole camp. He had operated on the camp commandant's daughter and saved her life when she was dying of peritonitis. He even had NKVD officers for patients; they came all the way from Gorky to see him. He was afraid of no one.

"If you understand, what are you waiting for?"

The secretary left.

"So." Dr. Teliants returned to the game. "I see you're playing by the rules tonight—"

Soon there was another knock on the door. The secretary was back, in a state of frightened agitation, with the same list.

"Doctor, the Representative says that he forbids you to send this man, that you must cross out this name or else you must go to see him personally at once . . . That's what he said."

---

6. "Zek" is a slaug term for a prisoner, from *zakluchenny*.

Dr. Teliants got up. His swarthy, sharply etched face with its thick black eyebrows under a shock of black hair wore a look of such fury that the woman fell back a step. He spoke to her softly, slowly, with exaggerated precision.

"Please tell the citizen Operational Representative that, as far as I am aware, I am still the chief surgeon of this hospital and hence am responsible for the hospital's patients. I have issued my instructions, and I don't propose to change them. I also don't propose to go to see him. I have an operation scheduled for an hour from now, and I am resting before the operation by playing a game of chess. That is my way of preparing myself. And for that reason I request that I be spared further interruptions. Is that understood?

"And another thing. If the citizen Operational Representative cancels my instructions, it will mean that he has become the chief surgeon in my place. In that event I shall stop working immediately, and the citizen Operational Representative can perform the operation himself—a case of appendicitis. And then an operation for hernia. One of his colleagues, by the way—the Operational Representative in Post No. 9."

He looked at his watch and continued. "In half an hour, I want to be informed if the transport has left. You don't have to come back yourself—send one of the orderlies. But don't forget to let me know. Otherwise the citizen Operational Representative will have a few operations on his hands. Is *that* understood? Now, good night."

He sat down and studied the chessboard. "You're not paying attention. You've lost your knight."

The transport left on time. Later that night our telephone operator spoke with the operator at Post No. 18—both men were zeks—and expressed particular interest in the health of one of the men in the new batch, hinting at his role.

A month passed. By then I was working as a male nurse. One evening, when I was on duty, Edith came in.

"Do you remember Stepan—the one who got Aunt Dusia transferred? They just brought him in. Fractures of both legs and spinal column. A tree fell on him."

Was it an accident or the outcome of the telephone call? I never knew.

II.

LEV RAZGON

Although of humble background—he was born in a small town in Belarus in 1908—Lev Razgon had the good fortune, or perhaps the misfortune, to have worked his way into the heart of the Soviet elite by the 1930s. A successful journalist, he married the daughter of Gleb Boky, one of the founders of the Cheka, the earliest incarnation of the Soviet secret police. As a result he was on intimate terms with many of the first generation of Bolshevik leaders. In 1937, when Stalin's great purge began and the Revolution turned on its own creators, he watched these leaders disappear one by one: his father-in-law, his wife's family members, his friends. He and his wife, Oksana, were arrested in 1938. She died in a transit prison before arriving at the camps. He went on to spend eighteen years in the Gulag. Released in 1956, Razgon rejoined the Party, as so many others did: it was a way to fit seamlessly back into Soviet society. But at the first opportunity, in 1988, he published several collections of memoirs—many written in secret years earlier—and renounced his Party membership. In his later years, Razgon became well known in Moscow as one of the founders of the historical and human rights society Memorial and a popular writer.

The excerpt that follows is from a chapter in his memoirs titled "Jailers." By "jailers," however, Razgon did not "just mean the individual who walks through the prison corridor with a bunch of keys" or the young armed guards who walked around the camp perimeter at night. What interested him was the psychology of the men and women who made decisions about prisoners' lives, sometimes without much guidance from Moscow. Information from the archives has confirmed that prison guards and camp authorities were rarely told directly to be cruel to the inmates: on the contrary, their official instructions were to keep prisoners fed and healthy, the better to do the required work. But most of those in positions of authority had already been degraded by years of service in the secret police and were dissatisfied with their lot: jobs in the Gulag were considered the worst in the secret service, and many officers were sent there as a kind of punishment.

More to the point, most did not consider their prisoners human: they were "enemies" or "criminals," units of labor to be deployed at the workplace, and therefore they did not require kindness or consideration at all. Nevertheless, the differences in their individual characters could have an enormous impact on the prisoners, as Razgon explains.

Jailers

Since jailers are at least originally human they each retain certain unique traits of character. The jailers whom I shall now describe were not all alike. They varied greatly in rank and ability. Among them were both the clever and the stupid, good and evil men, the bureaucrats and the fanatics. I and millions of others were at their mercy. I shall tell about my jailers. Let others tell about theirs. I think it is useful for all those who do not share our experience and knowledge to be told these things.

IVAN ZALIVA

Our transport walked for a whole week. Behind us lay the unmetaled dirt road to Knyazhpogost, the unfinished railway from Knyazhpogost to Vesliana, and the large wooden gates on the unballasted road over which there rose something like a triumphal arch bearing the handsome inscription, "Ustvymlag NKVD USSR." Behind us lay the transit camp and Camp No. 11, the Zimka outpost, and the Machinery Depot. Now we were walking along a broad, sandy roadway, which climbed up one hill after another. A pine forest of exceptional beauty stood on either side. The smooth bronze trunks reached up to the sky and between them the ground was covered with an even, silvery-velvet carpet that I had never seen before. It was reindeer moss. We were tired after a week on our feet, and so were our escorting guards. They no longer gave us the usual ten minutes' rest after two hours of marching, they cursed more often when prodding those who lagged behind, and they were in a hurry to hand us on to other masters.

Finally, after a sharp turn in the road, a river glistened ahead of us. It flowed rapidly over the shoals and calmly in the backwaters. Vesliana. A beautiful name, perhaps of early Slavonic origin. On the far side of the river stood an architectural structure to which our eyes were already quite accustomed: the tall logs, set upright in the ground, the posts of the compound fence; beyond them the low barracks; some way off, the unattractive houses of the camp administrators and free workers; the long stable building and the smoky chimney of the bakery . . . Our column crawled slowly across the pontoon bridge and approached the entrance to the camp. Various people stood outside the gates. Sharp young men in brand-new quilted work jackets held clean plywood slates and pencils in their hands: the work distributors. Other individuals in white coats who looked like prisoners—evidently doctors. The jailers and camp escort guard, who were not dressed up or there for show. And, in front of them all, a tall man in a well-made overcoat, with a blue NKVD cap and boots polished to an unbelievable shine. Wound about with the straps of his shoulder belt, his hand firmly placed on the wooden butt of his Mauser, he surveyed us with a condescending but severe gaze. This was our first camp boss, the head of Camp No. 1 in Ustvymlag, Senior Lieutenant Ivan Zaliva.

I am writing about him not only because he was my first jailer in the camps but because he was also a curious phenomenon. It was the first time I had come across someone of his kind, and for several years I was able to follow his career. The personality of Zaliva affected the many and, for us, very important changes then taking place in the camps. I do not know about Zaliva's biography before he came to the Gulag—where he had studied or worked earlier, and how he had reached the by no means insignificant rank of senior lieutenant in State Security. He was a man of astounding ignorance and rare stupidity. In these respects he stood out among the camp bosses, and they were not a profession known for exceptional wit and education. He did not steal, like most of his colleagues. Neither was he a despot: on the contrary, he kept strictly to his instructions. Zaliva was no sadist and when, during -40 degrees of frost, bound and completely naked "refusers"[1] were taken on sledges to the punitive outpost, he would follow their departure with sad regret in his eyes. He even had a certain Ukrainian kindheartedness and cheerfulness about him, tempered by the strictness necessary for his post.

Zaliva always tried to do what his superiors demanded. When they required that he accept as many zeks as possible, he agreed to take one transport after another. Unlike some camp directors he did not try to refuse new prisoners on the grounds that there were insufficient barracks, tents, clothes, tools, or food. The interests of the state governed all his activities. He crossed rice, semolina, and sorghum off the list

---

1. Prisoners who would not, or more likely could not, work.

of cereals supplied by the food depot and replaced them with cheap barley chaff; salt beef and horsemeat were replaced with dried cod; he would check the prices of medicines and demand cheaper substitutes. Instead of new expensive coats and felt boots he eagerly accepted second- and even thirdhand clothing from the depot. He took great care, though, of the camp's most valuable possession, its horses. Early each morning he himself would walk round the stable and make sure that they were being fed with the scarce oats. He checked how the feed was weighed out and given to the animals. While Zaliva continued to visit the stable the prisoners could not get their hands on this ration: the strict and incorruptible head of the camp would look on as the horses munched their oats. In the monthly reports from all the camps in Ustvymlag the lowest wastage levels for horses were consistently recorded at Camp No. 1. Zaliva was always praised for this.

To begin with, no one checked what he did with his "contingent" of zeks. During our first year in Camp No. 1, from 1938 to 1939, the transports arrived one after another, and Zaliva was held up as an exemplary boss who always found room for new "contingents." The explanation was simple: in his camp, places were rapidly freed. There were 517 in our Moscow transport, which reached his camp in late August 1938. By spring the next year only 27 of those Muscovites remained. About 20–30 people were, probably, transferred to other camps in Ustvymlag where their professional skills were put to use. All the rest died that first winter. The same fate awaited those then transported from Smolensk, Stavropol, and Mogilev.

In November 1938, 270 Chinese were driven to our camp from the Far East. They were inhabitants of Manchuria, clad in enormous wolfskin fur hats, long fur coats, and peculiar quilted boots of their own design. Each summer they had been accustomed, for years uncounted, to cross the invisible border with Russia and work as market gardeners until the winter. In 1937 and 1938 they were all arrested, given eight years for "illegal crossing of the frontier," and sent to the camps. Zaliva could not find sufficient words to express his delight. He set them hauling timber by hand. Usually horses pulled the felled trunks to the roadways, where they were carted away. There were few horses, however, and they were valuable; moreover, special paths had to be cleared for them at the work site. It was much easier to use manpower. Depending on the weight, a team of six, eight, or ten men lifted the trunk onto their shoulders and carried it. I have done the work and know what it's like. Your eyes strain from their orbits, and as you walk, all thoughts except one fly from your head: how to drop this terrible, crushing, and murderous burden as quickly as possible. None of us could take more than a week of such work. The Chinese, steadily, quietly, and calmly, worked day after day. Each of them took a pole in his free hand, carefully using it to test out the path ahead. Ten men carried a log that weighed almost two tons, and carried it very well, with great care.

They were good-hearted, honest, and hardworking men, the Chinese. Even in the camp they managed to keep as clean as was possible. For a month or more Lizarevich[2] and I lived in the Chinese barrack, and it was a joy to be there: there was no robbing or stealing, and it was always swept clean. The Chinese came back from work when it was pitch dark, ate the thin soup, and then repaired their torn fur clothing. (Zaliva had economized here too, since they did not then require camp issue.) They would sit on their heels on the bed boards and, holding the lighted splinter (then the only source of illumination) in their mouths, deftly and quickly sew up their fur coats. By February 1939, 269 of these Chinese had died. Only one remained alive, working in the kitchen.

Every day Zaliva called in the work distributor and the planner and asked for a detailed and strict account of the morning roll call. How many Group A (workers), he asked, how many in Group B (services in the compound), and how many in Group C (excused on grounds of illness)? He would check carefully that all these figures fell within the limits laid down by the Ustvymlag authorities. Only after that did he inquire about the night's "C figures." This meant those who had died. Higher authority did not set any limits for this category and, therefore, did not expect reports on them. During our first winter the daily "C figures" amounted to about 25–30 people. There were no particular diseases

2. A fellow inmate.

involved. It was simply that Zaliva strictly enforced all the instructions. A transport arrived and for the first three days, until the new prisoners began working, they were given the standard food allowance. Then they were transferred to an output-related diet. Even experienced and trained lumbermen, with good tools, found it difficult to fulfil the norm. For those unused to hard physical labor, weakened by prison and transfers, and lacking the right clothes or footwear, they were quite unattainable. After the three days all those who had just arrived found themselves on the punitive ration—300 grams [10½ ounces] of half-baked black bread, and two bowls of thin gruel a day. Nothing else. A week, ten days, or two weeks later, people began to swell up strangely, and then, over two to three days, an uncontrollable diarrhea would finish them off.

Before my eyes good-natured, bluff Zaliva killed off 1,500 people in the course of a single winter. Perhaps, even more. Yet, amazingly enough, the prisoners treated him with a kind of humorous disdain, and without hatred. To a great extent, we judged our jailers by how easily they could be hoodwinked. The stupidity, ignorance, and cowardice of Zaliva offered considerable opportunities. He prevented the prisoners from stealing the horses' oats only for as long as he continued to visit the stable.

"I can't help admiring your bravery, citizen director!" the vet said one day, with respect and a certain mournful pity in his voice.

"Indeed," Zaliva agreed condescendingly. "But why did you say that?" he suddenly inquired, pale with fear.

"Well, just think what our horses are sick with! In-fectious anemia . . ."

"You damn Trotskyist!" howled Zaliva. "Why didn't you tell me right away there was something contagious?!"

He never set foot in the stable again.

In accordance with an old instruction, never revoked, 58-ers[3] could not be permitted to work within the compound. Zaliva not only forbade us to be work distributors and managers but also quartermasters, ledger clerks in Supplies, bakers, and medical or barrack orderlies. All these posts were filled by the "socially acceptable," as thieves, robbers, rapists, and other criminals were termed in that instruction. Naturally, in such circumstances, the workers did not even receive half of a ration that had already been cut in the interests of the state. The most unbridled thievery and lawlessness reigned among the prisoners.

Yet it was under Zaliva's rule that the "politicals," the 58-ers, began their irreversible takeover of the camps. Only during the first winter did Zaliva flourish. At that time no one demanded that he meet the plan for timber supplies. A year later, when the peak of excess zeks had passed, Moscow firmly told the camps that they must not only guard their zeks but also give "performance": this was the term applied in official documents to the labors of millions of prisoners.

It was then that the formerly clear and precise distinction between what was permissible and what was not began to

3. Prisoners sentenced under Article 58—that is, for political crimes.

blur for Zaliva. In order to retain the goodwill of his superiors he needed clever planners and accountants, experienced engineers, capable organizers, and honest warehousemen. He could only find them among the "politicals." Zaliva's sense of self-preservation was so developed and strong, it turned out, that he began to send the "socially acceptable" on gang labor out into the forest and appoint to all the decisive posts those recommended by the head of planning, the chief accountant, and the doctor. The foreman and the planner blatantly exploited Zaliva's stupidity. They concealed almost half of the already very modest output, and after the daily report, Zaliva, pale with fright, would not summon the planner but himself run into the planning office and, stuttering, beg him almost obsequiously to "throw in" a few more dozens or hundreds of cubic meters . . . By nighttime the formerly fearsome and self-confident boss became a pitiful wretch, sweating from terrible fear. For now, every night, the administration called up each camp in turn for a report.

At about midnight the most important figures in the camp would gather in Zaliva's office. The director sat behind the lavish desk made for him by his own personal cabinetmaker, surrounded by jailers of various rank—the head of the guard, the "godfather," or security officer, and the heads of the medical and culture units. A little way off sat the prisoner heads of sections—the planner, accountant, norm-setter, works inspector, and the foremen. It was at the latter that Zaliva now gazed, with fear, suffering, and hope in his eyes. How he was probably cursing that damned radio and the prisoner, a radio operator, who had so skillfully and quickly set up the equipment and, if need arose, was sitting here to correct any defects in transmission.

All sat, talking in a whisper, as if they might be overheard by their yet more powerful bosses, at this very moment assembled in Vozhael at Ustvymlag headquarters, and sitting in the awesome director's office. Zaliva could not take his mournful, doglike eyes off the little box sitting on his desk. Finally, it began to crackle, gasp, and clear its throat. The voice of the head of production could suddenly be heard, calling all the camps participating in this roll-call report. Then the calmly insolent voice of the director himself rang out of the box. Since poor Zaliva was in charge of Camp No. 1, they began with him, and he was the butt of most of his superior's anger and zeal.

"Zaliva! Report on output!"

Zaliva's shaking voice was interrupted by a roar, "How much? How much? What are you up to there, you lazy good-for-nothings? What about the state plan? I sent you a contingent, and chucked in a few extra horses, now where's the output? I'll have you pile the logs on your prick, you idiot, and carry them here yourself!"

When Zaliva tried to interject a timid word of self-justification or a promise to do better in this stream of abuse he was shut up in such a way that even our experienced jailers began to look firmly at the floor. At last, this torment drew temporarily to a close: "If you don't raise output by 150 cubic meters [about 5,000 cubic feet] tomorrow I'll send you bare-assed into the forest to fetch the wood yourself! What else is left if you can't force your zeks to work!?"

Then the director turned to the other camps, more fortunate and, often, less fortunate. From time to time, he would remember Zaliva, "Are you there, Zaliva? You hear how they're working at No. 14? And they've less men, and fewer horses! They know how to make people work there. They know what the state plan means. They've probably organized a health resort at No. 1, since they can see what a fool their boss is!"

Yet Zaliva believed that he also knew how to make people work. He had often forced the doctors and all the camp "trusties" to go out and fell timber. But those cubic meters, where was he to make up those damned cubic meters?! Only by appealing to the "Trotskyists" could he get them. Zaliva pleaded an extra hundred cubic meters from the planner "for his own personal needs"; he agreed to let the foreman's mistress live in his cubicle with him; he was agreeable to anything, in fact, that could help him keep his difficult but still desirably superior position. Apart from the nightly radio reports there was also the daytime. Then he sat in his office, punishing and, where necessary, pardoning; he rode around the "work sites" on superb light sledges pulled by a pure-blooded ("anemic") trotter; and, having survived another twenty-four hours, he would sit down and calculate the day's profits and losses. For, apart from everything else, Zaliva was also unbelievably stingy. He was afraid to steal because he was almost as great a coward as he was a miser. He tried to spend as little as possible on himself and his wife. His dinner came from the prisoners' kitchen, to be "tried first" by him. Since the meal he received was always filling and delicious he took away the unconsumed part for his wife to eat. Even his bread was brought from the bakery "for testing." When his wife, nevertheless, had to pay for his food ration—it couldn't be allowed to go to waste!—she wrote down the quantity and price of each item. Zaliva would then come to the accountant's office with this slip of paper and check for himself that she hadn't cheated him. Sometimes he would weigh out the food again. Everything in his house was under lock and key, and Zaliva took the keys with him. In the morning he handed his wife the food she needed to survive the day.

As the value of those working in the camps rose, comparatively, and the demands for output continually increased, Zaliva was steadily demoted. He was made deputy director, then sent to a small camp producing skis, and then somewhere else. Toward the end of the war I came across him in charge of a small outpost of another camp. After the war ended he discharged himself and sold off all his belongings. The prisoners were able to buy a few worn-out greatcoats and his large ginger cat. Zaliva bargained long and passionately with the zeks, listing all his pet's exceptional qualities . . .

He returned to the Ukraine, taking with him his tormented wife, vast trunks packed with goodness knows what, and a fat pile of banknotes earned over years of zealous and loyal service to the state. He did not leave any friends behind him at Camp No. 1, but he bore no one any malice. Several months later, the chief of the escort guards received a contented and self-satisfied letter. They had appreciated him, after all, wrote Zaliva: he had been put in charge of a district MGB section in his own Poltava Region, and not sent back to the ferocious and tedious North.

. . .

COLONEL TARASIUK

"Only the first ten years are terrible. After that, you get used to it." Apart from gallows humor there is a good deal of truth in this common camp saying. Under more-or-less routine conditions a zek who survived two to three years had a chance of serving out his whole sentence. By the summer of 1941 we were already calm and settled camp regulars. Those who couldn't stand it became part of the night's "C figures." The survivors adapted and grew accustomed to the work; they established contact with their relatives outside and regularly received letters and parcels. By then we had made firm contact with other prisoners: we were friendly with some, and others were already almost family. We received many books from Moscow, and some of us were allowed to move about without an escorting guard. Zaliva was demoted, and the new bosses proved more reasonable. In their attempts to get more out of the prisoners they realized that it made sense to feed them better. It didn't require particular intelligence or humanitarian enlightenment to grasp this truth: most of the bosses were former peasants and they knew how to look after livestock.

This went on until June 22, 1941, the day Hitler attacked the Soviet Union. The shock affected all without exception and among the bosses led to an idiotically pointless burst of warning and preventative measures. During the very first day of war all radio amplifiers were taken down, correspondence and newspapers were forbidden, and no more parcels were allowed. The working day was extended to ten and, by some enthusiasts, to twelve hours. All days off work were also canceled. And of course they immediately introduced very severe cuts in the food given to the zeks.

By autumn people were beginning to be struck down by pellagra. It was the first time we had heard this awful word. With horror we began to observe in ourselves the primary and then progressive symptoms of the "disease of despair," as even the medical textbooks call it. The skin on our elbows became dry and rough and it peeled; dark spots appeared on our knuckles and rapidly turned black; around our throats a dark ring of patches blending with one another became ever clearer. Then followed a rapid loss of weight and uncontrollable diarrhea. That was almost the end. The diarrhea removed the mucous lining of the intestine, and it could not be restored. Nothing could bring someone back to life after that.

Within two to three months the camp was full of living skeletons. Only in the photographs presented by the prosecution at the Nuremberg trials have I seen such a degree of emaciation. Indifferent and without any will to live, corpselike figures covered by a taut gray skin sat on the board beds and calmly waited for death. Carts and then sledges carried the almost weightless bodies to the cemetery each morning. By spring of 1942 the camp had ceased to work

altogether. It was difficult to find people still able to cut firewood and bury the dead.

And here the military enthusiasm of the camp administration was exposed as being quite inappropriate. The war
could not be fought, they discovered, without timber. It
was needed for building airplanes, for making skis and pit-
props. Most important of all, it was essential for explosives.
Cellulose is the basis of all modern gunpowders and it is
obtained, as everyone knows, from wood pulp. No matter
how great their need for more soldiers at the front, timber-
industry workers were almost all exempted from service.
Our bosses were also exempted—but they couldn't supply
the timber required of them: there was no one to cut it . . .
Only then did their NKVD superiors start to do the mini-
mum that reason required. Timber-felling zeks began to be
fed as much as free workers. Correspondence was restored,
the amplifiers were put back, and newspapers started to
arrive. Prisoners were the only people in the country who
were allowed to receive food parcels. The old bosses were
quickly removed and others sent in to replace them.

It was then that we first heard the name of the new boss
of Ustvymlag, Colonel Tarasiuk.

At this time the remaining prisoners from the evacuated
Berezlag[4] joined our camp. When they described the man
who had been their boss and was now to head all of Ustvymlag, they would give a very significant shake of the head

4. A camp in the Urals, evacuated during World War II.

and explain that Tarasiuk was the worst bastard of all. (The word they actually used, following the peculiar jargon of the camps, was *pederast,* but it meant misanthrope rather than sexual deviant.) The former Berezlag prisoners also recounted at length the colonel's staggering administrative abilities. Yet they could not keep silent about this other, still more vividly pronounced, side to his character.

In fact, Tarasiuk represented the most extreme and fully developed type of slave owner. Before working in the camps, it was said, he had been in charge of Internal Affairs in Dagestan, in the north Caucasus, and was later removed from that prestigious post for "excesses." If he was really in Dagestan in 1937, then it becomes understandable why a column of centenarian Caucasians could appear at Kotlas while we were in transit there. I do not exaggerate. An entire trainload of old men aged eighty and more suddenly arrived in the Russian North from Dagestan. They did not know any Russian and expressed no desire to mix with anyone else or say how they came to be there. They sat silently on their heels with their eyes closed, in their homespun clothes and distinctive tall shaggy fur hats. Only when it was time to pray to Mecca did they rouse themselves from this immobility. They had been "withdrawn" from Dagestan, explained the zeks who hung around Distribution, as part of the elimination of feudal survivals. Many Dagestanis did not recognize the Soviet courts and preferred to go to the elders, who would judge them according to *adat,* their own customs and traditions. In order to reorient the republic's inhabitants toward more progressive forms of justice, all the old men were rounded up and given ten years apiece. Then they were sent to the North to die. This certainly bore the hallmark of Colonel Tarasiuk.

Now Tarasiuk was in charge of our camp, and we soon felt his purposeful and iron will. He traveled around all of Ustvymlag and drove the criminals out of any work linked with food, replacing them only with "politicals." The ledger clerks in Supplies, the quartermasters, and the cooks grew pale with fear when Tarasiuk appeared. Those who could work in the forest were even better fed than their escorting guards and the free workers. Medicines appeared and non-prisoner doctors arrived. Special anti-pellagra rations were introduced. Tarasiuk restored the capacity of the camp to work with all the energy of a gifted and determined administrator. But the methods he used!

I first saw him at close range when he visited us in spring 1942. Accompanied by a vast entourage of bosses of all ranks, he examined everything in the camp, including the latrines. If he came across someone working in the office or doing another job inside, and it seemed to him that person was fit enough to cut timber and not idle about in the compound, he beckoned the unfortunate with a flexing of his finger (rather like the mythical giant Viy in Gogol's tale).[5] The name of the unlucky zek was immediately written down on the work distributor's plywood slate. In the evening Tarasiuk summoned the section heads. I was then standing

5. The folklore giant Viy, the chief of the gnomes, appears in a story by Nikolai Gogol.

in for the senior norm-setter, and so, with all the prisoner-administrators (head of planning, chief accountant, works inspector, foremen, vets, and doctors), I found myself next to Tarasiuk.

He had the face of a Roman patrician, and a coldly calm and indifferent look. The way he sat down in the camp director's armchair, lifted the telephone receiver, and ordered the switchboard operator to connect him with headquarters—and the way he then spoke with them—all conveyed that he had been accustomed to giving orders for many years. He was used to having the power of life and death over those around him. The last phrase should be understood in the most literal sense. Moreover, it applied to the free workers just as much as the prisoners. The free workers were all exempted from fighting. Tarasiuk merely had to say, "Remove their exemption," and any of the bosses could be sent straight into battle. Telegrams "regretting to inform . . ." came for them with astonishing rapidity, as Tarasiuk was well aware.

He ordered the camp director to report on the condition of his "contingent," as the prisoners were termed in all official documents. Breathless with nerves, our boss listed how many of our zeks were fit "for any work," for "medium," or for "light" work; how many were in the weak team and in the sickbay. How many of them worked in the forest, in the office, and doing other jobs around the compound.

Tarasiuk listened calmly and negligently to this report. Suddenly he interrupted, "How many bonus meals are handed out in the compound?"

A "bonus meal" meant a little runny porridge, which was poured onto a wooden platter and cooled to form something like a jelly. The administrative and technical staff got it as well as the tree fellers and all those service personnel who did piecework, such as the laundry workers and water carriers. After hearing the reply, Tarasiuk calmly said, "Cut it. Use it to increase the amount for those working in the forest."

The head of General Supplies wanted to say something, but Tarasiuk almost imperceptibly flashed his eyes at the man, who swallowed his words and kept quiet.

"And who are those? What did you call them?" inquired Tarasiuk.

He was referring to the "convalescent team." There were 246 of them in our camp. Our boss looked at Dr. Kogan, who was the acting head of Health and Sanitation. Still young, Kogan had been sent to work in the camps after being wounded at the front. He stood up and, not without some pride, said that these people had been "plucked from the grips of pellagra." We could now be sure none of them would die . . . The following dialogue ensued:

> *Tarasiuk:* What are they getting?
>
> *Kogan:* They are all receiving the anti-pellagra ration established by the Gulag Health and Sanitation department (and he specified the quantity of proteins in calories).
>
> *Tarasiuk:* How many of them will go out to work in the forest, and when?
>
> *Kogan:* Well, none of them will ever go to work in the forest again, of course. But now they'll survive, and it will be possible to use them for light work within the compound.

Tarasiuk: Stop giving them any anti-pellagra rations. Write this down: these rations are to be given to those working in the forest. The other prisoners are to get the disability rations.

Kogan: Comrade Colonel! Obviously I didn't explain clearly. These people will only survive if they're given a special ration. A disabled prisoner receives 400 grams [14 ounces] of bread. On that ration they'll be dead in ten days. We can't do that!

Tarasiuk looked at the upset doctor, and there was even a sign of interest on his face. "What's the matter? Do your medical ethics prevent you from doing this?"

"Of course, they do . . ."

"Well, I don't give a damn for your ethics!" said Tarasiuk calmly, and with no indication whatsoever of anger. "Have you written that down? Let's move on . . ."

All 246 died within a month.

We had both clever and stupid, kind and cruel camp bosses. Tarasiuk was something quite different. He resembled in some ways the slave owners of classical times. The idea that his slaves were human beings never worried or concerned him. I said that his face recalled that of a Roman patrician. And he lived like a Roman who has been appointed governor of some barbarous newly conquered province. Vegetables and fruit and flowers quite alien to the North, were grown for him in special hothouses and orangeries. The best cabinetmakers were found to make his furniture. The most famous couturiers of the recent past dressed his capricious and willful wife. When he felt unwell he was not examined by some freely hired little doctor who had sold himself to the Gulag as a medical student. No, Tarasiuk was treated by professors who had headed the biggest Moscow clinics and were now serving their long sentences in the medical barracks of remote forest camps.

The Roman matrons, as we know, stripped naked in front of male slaves not because they were shameless but because they did not consider those slaves to be human beings. Tarasiuk, like these figures from antiquity, lacked any similar inhibitions. Moreover, he showed it not only in front of the zeks but also of the free workers, who, in origin and situation, hardly differed from the prisoners. Once he gathered all the norm-setters and economists together at headquarters in Vozhael for the latest "bawling out." It was the middle of the war, when the ration of even the free workers could sustain a semi-starved existence only with difficulty. The meeting had gone on for a long time, and people were sitting exhausted and worn out from hunger. Suddenly well-dressed young waitresses in lace pinafores and with silk grips in their hair entered the room.

Tarasiuk was seated, as was the custom, in front of us behind a separate table. With professional speed and in silence the waitresses covered it with a spotlessly white cloth, stiff with starch. Then they laid out various-sized dishes in front of the colonel. Without interrupting the meeting Tarasiuk tucked a dazzling white napkin into the stiff collar of his uniform and uncovered the dishes. The delicious smell of some wildfowl prepared by his personal cook (formerly chef in a famous Saint Petersburg restaurant) wafted over the room. We felt faint. Indifferently Tarasiuk bolted the fowl, only interrupting this activity to roar imperiously at someone or cut another short with an intimidating glance of his clear, cold eyes. So little idea had he that those before him were in any respect his equals that he could have performed any physical function in front of us, if it proved more convenient for him. It would be difficult, moreover, to call him particularly vicious.

He encouraged zeks who worked well. Those who broke production records were allowed to take women to their barracks without fearing the warders. After doctors and tailors had visited him in his mansion the cook would take them out a slice of white bread spread with butter ... An unbending order was maintained throughout Ustvymlag under which those who could cut timber lived well, and those who could not, irrespective of the reason, suffered. There was order. There was even a kind of justice, if one can use that word in this context. For the camp bosses were careful not to be tyrannous under Tarasiuk, and did not steal from the prisoners—they gave them what they were due. And this meant, we found out, that we should have mattresses and even sheets. They appeared from somewhere, and the prisoners slept in sheets. Truly, he was a just boss!

We hated none of the bosses like we hated Tarasiuk. Fortunately he was only with us for a short while. Once Ustvymlag was working properly again he was transferred to put another camp back on its feet.

*   *   *

When Rika[6] and I found ourselves free at last we lived in Stavropol. There we went hungry all the time and counted each kopeck. One day Rika gave me her last three rubles, and I went to Stalin Avenue to buy garlic sausage and bread. In the shop next door they sold newspapers which had come by the evening train. Usually I just read the copy of *Pravda* hung up in the showcase by the concert hall. My eyes lighted on *Izvestiya*, however, and a familiar surname in a black frame at the bottom of the last page made my heart almost stop. I bought the paper. "With deep sorrow the Chief Administration of the Timber Industry Camps announces that after a severe and protracted illness, the great organizer and award-bearer Colonel Tarasiuk . . ."

I went into the food shop and instead of sausage bought a 250-gram [9-ounce] bottle of vodka and some bread with the remaining thirty kopecks. When I reached home I held out the newspaper to Rika as she looked at my purchases with incomprehension. I watched as her tired and worn-out face lit up with an irrepressible triumph! We sat at the table, cut up the bread, and poured out the vodka. Rika did not drink as a rule, but now she didn't even pretend to pour more into my glass. Sighing with relief that Tarasiuk had died, and probably in terrible pain (he must have suffered!), we drank all the vodka . . . He was dead and we . . . we were free. So there was Justice after all! Or a God? I don't know what to call it. Anyway, that's not important. The thing is, it exists.

6. Rika Berg, Razgon's second wife.

12

ANATOLY MARCHENKO

Today's camps for political prisoners are just as horrific as in Stalin's time. A few things are better, a few things are worse . . ." So began Anatoly Marchenko's *My Testimony*. When it first began to circulate in Moscow in the late 1960s this memoir deeply shocked the city's intelligentsia, most of whom had believed that the Soviet Union's labor camps had closed for good.

Born in 1938, the working-class son of illiterate parents, Marchenko received his first prison conviction for hooliganism. He received his second conviction in 1961 for treason: he had tried to escape the Soviet Union by crossing the border into Iran. He was thus condemned to serve his second, political sentence in Dubrovlag, Morodovia, one of the harshest post-Stalinist political camps. He also spent time in Vladimir, another political prison noted for its punitive conditions.

Many elements of Marchenko's prison experience would have seemed familiar to people who had heard stories of

Stalin's camps. The numbers were smaller: in the 1960s there were far fewer prisoners—tens of thousands rather than millions. Nevertheless, just like his Stalin-era predecessors, Marchenko rode to Morodovia in a crowded train wagon. Also like his predecessors, he received a loaf of bread, forty grams (one and a half ounces) of sugar, and a salted herring to last him the trip. Access to water depended on which soldier was in charge of the train: "If he's a good one he'll bring you two or three kettles, but if he can't be bothered to fetch and carry for you, then you can sit there until you die of thirst."

At the camp, Marchenko found the same generalized hunger, if not the same level of starvation, there would have been in the past. His daily food rations consisted of 700 grams (25 ounces) of bread, 450 grams (1 pound) of usually rotten vegetables, 85 grams (3 ounces) of usually spoiled cod, and 55 grams (2 ounces) of meat. By contrast, the dogs guarding the prisoners received 450 grams of meat. By his second term, "strict-regime prisoners"—which included all the political dissidents—were required to wear numbers on their uniforms, just as they had done in the 1940s, which they considered a symbol of their dehumanization.

But there were new elements to prison life as well. By the 1960s, Soviet criminal culture had become even further degraded. The criminal gangs had split into factions and "families" for self-protection and adopted a violent culture of homosexual rape and domination. Many people who were mentally ill wound up being sent to political prisons. Marchenko describes them too.

The selection that follows is about another kind of camp experience, however: the punishment cell, or "cooler," an institution present in the Stalin era and long afterward. Prisoners were sent to the cooler for defying camp regulations, for rudeness to the commandants, or sometimes for no particular reason. Though conditions varied from place to place and era to era, certain aspects were always the same: cold, lack of bedding, meager rations. Marchenko writes that by the time he had spent seven days in the cooler, he was "eager" to return to the relatively luxurious regime of the camp.

The Cooler

I had caught a chill in the Karaganda camps already and had received no treatment. Since then I had suffered from a chronic inflammation of both ears, which from time to time would become acute. This time it was also my ears that caused the trouble. My head was splitting in two; I had shooting pains in my ears; it was difficult to fall asleep at night and painful to open my mouth at meals. On top of that I had fits of nausea and dizziness.

I went to the camp medical post, although the old hands warned me that it was useless, that the ear specialist came once a year and summoned everyone who had complained of ear trouble during the past year to come to him at the same time. There were quite a few. "What's wrong?" "My ears." Without further ado the specialist would note it down in his notebook and write out a prescription for hydrogen peroxide. No further inquiries and no proper examination, and there was no chance of being excused from work—it was out of the question. Only if you turned out to have a high temperature would they consider excusing you from work for a few days.

I appealed to the doctor several times and each time heard only insulting assertions that since I didn't have a temperature I must be well and therefore was simply trying to dodge work. And at the end of June, for failing to fulfill my norm, I was given seven days in the P.C., or punishment cell—in other words, the cooler. I found nothing surprising in this: given that I was failing to fulfill my daily norm, the cooler was inevitable. At first they call you up in front of your company officer to listen to a sermon about every con having to redeem his sin in the eyes of the people by honest labor.

"Why didn't you fulfill your norm?" asks the officer when his homily is finished. This when he can see that the man in front of him can barely stand up. "Sick? How can you be when you've got no temperature! It's very bad to pretend, to dissimulate, to try and dodge your work." And just to make the point clear he gives you several days in the cooler.

Now what did the punishment cell look like in 1961? First there was an ordinary camp barrack block, divided into cells. The cells were various: some were for solitary, others for two people, five, or even twenty, and if necessary they would pack up to thirty or even forty in them. It was situated in a special regime camp about a quarter of a mile [half a kilometer] from Camp No. 10. A tiny exercise yard had been specially fenced off; it was pitted and trampled hard, and in it, even in summer, there was not a single blade of grass—the least shoot of green would be swallowed at once by the starving cons in the cooler.

The cells themselves were equipped with bare bunks consisting of thick planks—no mattresses or bedding were allowed. The bunks were short; you had to sleep bent double; when I tried to straighten out, my legs hung over the end. In the center of the bunk, running crosswise and holding the planks together, was a thick iron bar. Now what if this bar had been placed underneath the planks? Or set in a groove, if it had to be on top, so that it didn't stick out? But no, this iron bar, two inches [five centimeters] wide and almost an inch [three centimeters] thick, was left sticking up in the very middle of the bunk, so that no matter how you lay it was bound to cut into your body, which had no protection from it.

The window was covered with stout iron bars, and the door had a peephole. In one corner stood the prisoner's inseparable companion, the sloptank—a rusty vessel holding about twelve gallons [55 liters], with a lid linked to it by a stout chain. Attached to one side of the tank was a long iron rod threaded at the other end. This was passed through a special aperture in the wall and on the other side, in the corridor, the warder would screw a big nut onto it. In this way the sloptank was fixed immovably to the wall. During toilet break the nut would be unscrewed so that the cons could carry the tank out and empty it. This procedure took place daily in the morning. The rest of the time the sloptank stood in its appointed place, filling the cell with an unspeakable stench . . .

At 6:00 A.M. came a knocking at all doors: "Wake up! Wake up for toilet break!" They started taking us to get washed. At last it was our cell's turn. However, it was washing only in name. You had hardly had time to wet your hands when you were already being prodded from behind: "Hurry, hurry, you can get all the washing you want after you've been released!" Less than a minute is the regulation time for a con to wash in, and whoever fails to get washed has to rinse his face over the sloptank in the cell.

And so, back in our cell once more, we waited for breakfast—alas nothing but a name: a mug of hot water and a ration of bread—fourteen ounces [400 grams] for the whole day. For dinner they gave us a bowl of thin cabbage soup consisting of almost pure water, in which some leaves of stinking pickled cabbage had been boiled—though little enough even of that found its way into the bowl. I don't think even cattle would have touched this soup of ours, but in the cooler the con not only drinks it straight from the side of the bowl, but even wipes the bowl with his bread and eagerly looks forward to supper. For supper we got a morsel of boiled cod the size of a matchbox, stale and slimy. Not a grain of sugar or fat is allowed to prisoners in the cooler.

I hate to think what we prisoners were driven to by starvation in the cooler. Return to camp was awaited with even greater eagerness than the end of your sentence. Even the normal camp hunger rations seemed an unimaginable feast in the cooler. I hate to think how I starved in there. And it is even more horrible to realize that now, even as I write this, my comrades are still being starved in punishment cells . . .

The time drags agonizingly between breakfast and dinner and between dinner and supper. No books, no newspapers, no letters, no chess. Inspection twice a day and after dinner a half-hour walk in the bare exercise yard behind barbed wire—that's the extent of your entertainment. During inspections the warders take their time: the prisoners in each cell are counted and recounted and then checked with the number on the board. Then a meticulous examination of the cell is carried out. With big wooden mallets the warders sound out the walls, bunks, floor, and window bars to see whether any tunnels are being dug or any bars have been sawn through and whether the prisoners are planning to escape. They also check for any inscriptions on the walls. During the whole of this time the prisoners all have to stand with their caps off. . . .

During the thirty-minute exercise period you can also go to the latrines. If there are twenty of you in a cell, however, it is difficult to manage in time. There are two latrines; a line forms, and again you are chivvied: "Hurry, hurry, our time's nearly up, what are you sitting around for!" If you don't manage it, there's always the sloptank back in the cell, and they never let you out to go to the latrines again, not even if you're an old man or ill. Inside, during the day, the cell is stifling and stinks to high heaven. At night, even in summer, it is cold—the cell block is built of stone and the floor is cement: they are specially built that way so as to be as cold and damp as possible. There is no bedding and nothing to cover yourself with, except for your reefer jacket. This, like all your other warm clothes, is taken away when you are searched before being stuck in the cooler, but they give it back to you at night.

There is not the slightest chance of taking a morsel of food with you to the cooler, or even half a puff's worth of cigarette butt or paper or the lead of a pencil—everything is taken away when you are searched. You yourself and the underwear, trousers, and jacket that you are forced to take off are all poked and prodded through and through.

From ten o'clock at night till six in the morning you lie huddled on your bare boards, with the iron bar digging into your side and a cold damp draft from the floor blowing through the cracks between them. And you long to fall asleep, so that sleeping, at least, you can forget the day's torments and the fact that tomorrow will be just the same. But no, it won't work. And you can't get up and run about the cell: the warder will see you through the peephole. So you languish there, tossing and turning from side to side until it is almost light again; and no sooner do you doze off than: "Get up! Get up! Toilet break!"

Incarceration in the punishment cell is supposed to be limited to not more than fifteen days, but the officers can easily get round this rule. They let you out to go back to camp one evening and the next morning condemn you to another fifteen days. What for? A reason can always be found. You stood in your cell so as to block the peephole; picked up a cigarette butt during your exercise period (that one of your camp friends had tossed over the fence to you); answered a warder rudely ... Yes, you can get a further fifteen days for absolutely nothing at all. Because if you really rebel and allow yourself to be provoked into making a protest, you get not simply fifteen days in the cooler but a new trial by decree.

In Kargal I was once kept in the cooler for forty-eight days, being let out each time only so that a new directive could be read to me ordering my "confinement to a punishment cell." The writer Yuli Daniel[1] was once given two successive spells in the cooler at Dubrovlag Camp No. 11 for "swearing at a sentry"—this happened in 1966.

Some men can't bear the inhuman conditions and the hunger and end up by mutilating themselves: they hope they will be taken to hospital and will escape, if only for a week, the bare boards and stinking cell, and will be given more human nourishment. While I was in the cooler, two of the cons acted as follows: they broke the handles off their spoons and swallowed them; then, after stamping on the bowls of the spoons to flatten them, they swallowed these too. But even this wasn't enough—they broke the pane of glass in the windows and by the time the warders had managed to unlock the door each had succeeded in swallowing

---

1. The writer and dissident Yuli Daniel (1925–88) was the object of a notorious case of political persecution and a show trial.

several pieces of glass. They were taken away and I never saw them again; I merely heard that they were operated on in the hospital at Camp No. 3.

When a con slits his veins or swallows barbed wire, or sprinkles ground glass in his eyes, his cellmates don't usually intervene. Every man is free to dispose of himself and his life as best he can and in whatever way he wishes; every man has the right to put an end to his sufferings if he is unable to bear them any longer.

There is also usually one cell in the punishment block that is filled with people on hunger strike. One day, as a mark of protest, a con decides to go on hunger strike, so he writes out an official complaint (to the camp governor, the Central Committee, Khrushchev—it is all the same who to, it has absolutely no significance; it's simply that a hunger strike "doesn't count" without an official complaint, even if you starve to death anyway) and refuses to take any more food. For the first few days no one takes a blind bit of notice. Then, after several days—sometimes as many as ten or twelve—they transfer you to a special cell set aside for such people, and start to feed you artificially, through a pipe. It is useless to resist, for whatever you do they twist your arms behind your back and handcuff you. This procedure is carried out in the camps even more brutally than in the remand prison—by the time you've been "force-fed" once or twice you are often minus your teeth. And what you are given is not the feeding mixture that I got at Ashkhabad, but the same old camp skilly, only even thinner, so that the pipe doesn't get blocked. Furthermore the skilly you get in the cells is lukewarm, but in artificial feeding they try to make it as hot as possible, for they know that this is a sure way of ruining your stomach.

Very few men are able to sustain a hunger strike for long and get their own way, although I have heard of cases where prisoners kept it up for two to three months. The main thing is, though, that it's completely useless. In every instance the answer to the protest is exactly the same as to all other complaints, the only difference being that the governor himself comes to see the hunger striker, insofar as the enfeebled con is unable to walk:

"Your protest is unjustified, call off your hunger strike. Whatever you do, we won't let you die. Death would save you from your punishment, and your term isn't up yet. When you go free from here you are welcome to die. You have made a complaint, you are complaining about us to the higher authorities. Well, you can write away—it's your right. But all the same it is we who will be examining your complaint . . ."

And this was the sanatorium I had been sent to on account of my illness. I served my seven days and came out, as they say, holding onto the walls—they had worn me to a shadow. Nevertheless, despite my weakness, I still had to go out to work the next day in order not to earn myself another spell in the cooler.

13.

K. PETRUS

Petrus is a pseudonym for the author of a short but unusual Gulag memoir. *Prisoners of Communism* appeared in 1996 under the auspices of a publishing house linked to the Russian Orthodox Church. The memoir is valuable both because it is a relatively early account of the camps—Petrus was in Siblag, near Novosibirsk, in the mid-1930s—and also because it tells the story of a long imprisonment from the point of view of a deeply religious person. Petrus does not remember his years in the Gulag as a long torment but rather tells of conversions he effected, the people of faith he encountered, and his moments of revelation.

Nevertheless, the selection that follows was chosen not for its religious qualities but because it illuminates an aspect of camp life that has rarely been so well described: the strange ambiguity of "freedom." After many years in camps, surviving prisoners would eventually be released—but to what? Many no longer had living family members; some did not have a profession or trade. The return home was complicated and difficult: from remote places like the Kolyma peninsula released prisoners might wait weeks or months for a ferry to Vladivostok. Many already knew that they would not be allowed to live in their previous homes in Moscow or Saint Petersburg: they had been given a "wolf's ticket," a release document that required them to live at least a hundred kilometers (sixty miles) away from major cities. Some were assigned to exile villages in Kazakhstan or Central Asia.

As a result, many decided not to leave at all and remained on the edges of camps, employed by the Gulag administration as "free workers." Even after the Gulag itself ceased to exist—following Stalin's death, most of the camps were slowly closed—some former prisoners remained. They and their descendants still form an important part of the population of Russia's northern cities. Petrus decided to leave, but the journey was not easy. Nor were his first encounters with Soviet citizens who had not shared his experience. Late at night, he explains, walking to a train station, he met a woman who asked him where he was from: "I'm from a place you'll probably never ever see." He already had the feeling that his camp experience had taken place in a different world, an alternate universe. And that, too, was typical.

Liberation

When my prison term was coming down to the wire or, as they say in the camps, "down to the bell," I had no illusions about what awaited me on the outside. The only thing that drew me there was my family, who were living in terrible privation. I was scared to death that a second sentence would be tacked onto the first, not because *I* would suffer but because my family would. For their sake, I had to get out and get back to them.

Usually, one month before a prisoner was freed, he was transferred to a central lagpunkt. Here he was processed for release. When I had only one month left to serve and still had not been transferred from N——k to K——sk[1] I began to get nervous. N——k housed only five hundred prisoners; many of them were also finishing out their sentences and were expecting to be transferred to K——sk. My ambiguous situation plunged my fellow prisoners into despair. If they can tack on a new sentence for one prisoner today, perhaps they will tack on one for everyone tomorrow?

So on my way to work in the kitchen or the baths I was constantly stopped and asked, "What's up, why aren't you getting moved to K——sk? You've got less than a month to go . . . Are they, what . . . adding on?"

---

1. Petrus did not name the camps he had lived in, perhaps for fear of re-arrest. He may also have been following the tradition found in nineteenth-century Russian literature of identifying places in this manner.

Anyone who has done time knows how fast it flies there. It flew by particularly swiftly in Soviet camps. My last week, however, dragged on slowly and painfully. But I knew that not a hair of my head would fall were it not God's will, and that faith sustained me. I knew that my freedom hinged on decisions made by Moscow and kept inventing various scenarios. I was supposed to be released on December 10, but as the date approached there were no signs, no signals. The camp administrators denied any knowledge; nothing but silence from Moscow.

But Providence was not so silent.

At ten o'clock one morning I was summoned to the main office and half an hour later was plunked onto a standard one guard–one horse sleigh and sent off to K——sk. We were expected to cover 120 kilometers [75 miles] in two days, and the driver—that is, me—pushed our lively little Siberian horse hard in order make the first shelter by nightfall. My guard, fearing a wolf attack, pushed me too: "Go. Go! Step it up!" Still, it was not until late in the evening that we reached our next stop. He hauled me to the local militia to transfer custody, but the chief countered that he had no special cells set aside for "transports" and he could not just lodge me in a cellar. He did not want to answer for "some frozen guy." They took me back to the station, where my guard and I slept in real beds, side by side.

We spent the second night in a dirty kolkhoz dooryard, along with the kolkhoznik.

The next morning another kolkhoznik walked up to us and proffering his hand said, "I think you might have dropped this little pouch, some money maybe. I found it out here." He looked at the guard, then at me. I fumbled in my pocket. It was empty. My last hundred rubles had disappeared. But this stranger had given them back.

I was so grateful! I gave him a firm handshake; he looked at us silently, his eyes moist. I saw and felt what he was going through, and felt glad both for myself and for him. It may be that he too was a believer, that he had guessed why I was standing there with an armed guard at my side. In those days a hundred rubles was not a lot of money, but that wasn't the point. The point was that the man had given it, and that both of us felt the joy of his gift.

We made it to K——sk by dinnertime the next day. This was the last stage on my road to freedom. As the guard turned me over to the camp authorities, he said, "Look, if all prisoners were like you, things might be different." But what this peasant boy from somewhere around Chernigov meant by *different* I never found out, because two warders immediately grabbed me and started patting me down.

On the thirteenth I was processed. On the fourteenth I was free.

As he was writing out my "passport to life"—the document that proved I had served out my sentence and that also determined my next place of residence—the official leafed through a very thick book, searching out an appropriate district for me.

I was later told that this fat book, which prisoners called the Talmud, was an index, a list of places where "counter-revolutionaries" who had served out their sentences were sent. The index was divided into chapters and sub-chapters based on Article 58. So I was banned from any capital, major city, industrial center, port, or border city, as well as from the district I had lived in before my arrest. All these bans and restrictions can be described by a single phrase: "forty below."

I was out, but was I free? As a "counter-revolutionary" with a stain on his record, I was restricted to a particular district, the better to feel the full force of the despotic regime. So that at any time I could be swept back behind bars. So that it would always be watching not only over my behavior but also over my soul.

At the guard post they frisked me one last time, reread my documents, then swung open the gate and let me out. I walked past the grim and filthy barracks where the so-called free workers, former kulaks, were housed, and struggled to figure out my place in all this.

"So I'm free?" I whispered to myself, not quite believing that I was on my way to the local militia to get myself an internal passport. I saw a haggard woman's face in one doorway in those barracks; she glanced at the dirty bundles heaved over both my shoulders and bobbed her head knowingly. I kept thinking that everyone was looking at me, that I would be stopped any minute now. But at the same time I felt that I could weather all these hardships, find my family and another life. I ducked around a corner, stopped to take a breath, looked up at the Siberian sky, and remembered the comfort of Psalm 27: "The Lord is my light and my salvation; whom shall I fear? The Lord is the strength of my life; of whom shall I be afraid?"

Both in the Zapoliarie camp and in N——k, many of my fellow prisoners had asked me to visit their families or send messages once I got outside. I had memorized about ten addresses. On their release, prisoners were searched meticulously, and the only way to pass along illegal information was to memorize it. The last time I was about to be frisked at the guardhouse, the guard on duty was strict: "Any letters to the outside?"

"No," I said calmly. I knew them all by heart.

"Addresses on the outside?"

"No.

"Well, what if we find some?"

"Go ahead and look."

"Fine. Beat it!"

And so I carried with me all the messages sent to the orphaned families, the pleas and wishes of their fathers, husbands, sons. Addresses flickered in my head: Irkutsk, X Street, no. 123; Tashkent, X Street, no. ??? ; Cheliabinsk, X Street, no. 17; Kharkov, X Street, no. 36; Stalingrad, X Street, no. 45, Moscow, Mayakovsky Square, no. X, Leningrad, Vasilievsky, Ostrov . . . The former editor of a major newspaper had asked me to write to his sister.

Meanwhile, here I was, lying on an upper berth in a third-class railcar speeding along the Trans-Siberian to Europe. It took eight days to get to Moscow, and all I wanted to do was eat. Eat and eat.

The only food for sale at the train stations was rotting pickles, a ruble apiece. Bread, let alone any other food, was impossible to find, although the war hadn't even started yet, if you didn't count the war with Finland, which was being waged exclusively by the "Leningrad Military District."

Somewhere along the way between Novosibirsk and the Urals, a *komandirsha*[2] sold me loaf of bread, and that sustained me a bit. She spied a "rabbit"[3] under her seat, summoned the chief conductor, and the raggedy young man was dragged out of the car. It turned out that he had escaped from a camp and was trying to make his way out of Siberia.

"So, you don't feel bad about turning him in?" I asked her as they led the escapee away.

"What's to feel bad about?" she replied tranquilly. She seemed surprised that I asked.

"Well if this were your brother or your husband, would you have done the same thing?" I asked, peering into her face.

"If they'd done something wrong of course I would have turned them in," she answered, unconcerned.

I said nothing, but thought, "Oh, this is Stalin's brood. Betray your father, mother, husband, child, anyone."

In Kazan I managed to buy another loaf of bread, which lasted until Moscow, where I was able to find more food.

That night I went looking for the engineer's family. Several metro stations down, I found the right street and the right building, took the elevator to the seventh floor, and

2. Railway conductor.
3. Freeloader.

tentatively pushed the buzzer next to a dark door with the right apartment number. An old woman peeped out, called the engineer's wife, and then the two of them examined me and my camp clothes.

"Are you the wife of N.?"

"Yes, I am, what do you want?"

"I have a request from your husband . . ."

It is hard to describe in words how surprised the women were. We went to the kitchen; a twelve-year-old boy wearing a red Pioneers[4] scarf ran in.

I briefly told her what my engineer friend N. had told me. The women were upset, crying. The Pioneer, his mouth agape, just stood there, fiddling with his scarf. In parting she offered me ten rubles for the road. I turned down the money, said my good-byes, took the elevator down, and found myself on the street again. I had to get to Kursk Station, and decided to go on foot.

I was striding along, and suddenly there in front of me a female figure loomed up. She was dragging an enormous suitcase. As I drew even with her, a velvety voice said, "Comrade, help me haul this case to the Kursk Station. I'll pay you for your trouble."

"Of course. I'm at your service."

I took the suitcase as she walked next to me, complaining. "I've been dragging it, dragging it, thought my arms

4. The Young Pioneer Youth Organization, a widespread scouting organization for young people aged ten to fifteen, was established by Lenin in 1922.

would fall off. You'd think someone would help. But now here you are! I'm so grateful for your courtesy." She stopped talking, then started up again, "No doubt you just got here too?"

"Right."

"From a long way away?"

"Yes."

"Where from, exactly?" she persisted.

"My dear, I'm from a place you'll probably never ever see," I answered. "I'm from another world entirely, where there's no good or evil, just pure pleasure."

"What . . . what did you say?" she squeaked, barely keeping up with my long strides. "What do you mean another world? . . . I don't understand."

"Of course you can't. If the NKVD couldn't understand me, then how in the world could you?" Nonplussed, she said nothing. Then, seeing the lights of the station ahead, she squeaked again, "Well, this is the end of our road. Take it over there, toward the doors, under the canopy. Good, yes . . . thank you. How much do I owe you for your work, citizen?"

"You don't owe me anything. You needed help. I helped you. It's awkward translating that into money. Have a safe trip!"

I dipped her a bow in parting, but she threw up her hands and exclaimed, "I've never met anyone so strange. You come from another world—you turn down money when you surely need it. I would have liked to get better acquainted. Well anyway, good-bye. Safe travels. You said you were going to the Caucasus? All the best."

And so we parted. It was eleven o'clock at night. Two hours later I was on the train to Sochi, heading south, where friends, family, and the blue air of the mountains awaited me.

I hardly dared dream of going home.

Acknowledgments

Translations of the texts by Elena Glinka, Anatoly Zhigulin, Nina Gagen-Torn, Isaak Filshtinsky, and K. Petrus are by Jane Miller.

Every reasonable effort has been made to secure permissions for previously published translations. If any errors should be noticed, please contact Yale University Press. Corrections will follow in subsequent editions.

Punctuation and spelling have been standardized throughout.

"Arrest," by Dmitry S. Likhachev, excerpted from Dmitry S. Likhachev, *Reflections on the Russian Soul: A Memoir,* copyright © 2000 by Central European University Press. Reprinted by permission of Central European University Press.

"Interrogation," by Alexander Dolgun, excerpted from Alexander Dolgun and Patrick Watson, *Alexander Dolgun's Story,* copyright © 1975 by Alexander Dolgun. Used by permission of Alfred A. Knopf, a division of Random House, Inc.

"The Kolyma Tram," by Elena Glinka, excerpted from Elena Glinka, *Oswenstim bez Pechei,* copyright © 1995 by Vozvraschenie. Used by permission of Vozvraschenie.

"A Day in Labor Corrective Camp No. 21," by Kazimierz Zarod, excerpted from Kazimierz Zarod, *Inside Stalin's Gulag,* originally published in 1990 by the Book Guild, Ltd.

"On Work," by Anatoly Zhigulin, excerpt from Anatoly Zhigulin, *Chyornie Kamni,* originally published in 1996 by Izdatelstvo Kultura.

"On Faith," by Nina Gagen-Torn, excerpted from Nina Gagen-Torn, *Memoria,* copyright © 1995 by Vozvraschenie. Used by permission of Vozvraschenie.

"Promotion," by Isaak Filshtinsky, excerpted from Isaak Filshtinsky, *My Shagayem pod Konvoyem,* copyright © 1994 by Vozvraschenie. Used by permission of Vozvraschenie.

"My Child," by Hava Volovich, excerpted from Hava Volovich, "My Past," in *Till My Tale Is Told: Women's Memoirs of the Gulag,* edited by Simeon Vilensky and translated by John Crowfoot, Marjorie Farquharson, Catriona Kelly, Sally Laird, and Cathy Porter, pp. 260–64. Copyright © 1999 Indiana University Press. Reprinted with permission of Indiana University Press and Vozvraschenie.

"The House of Meetings," by Gustav Herling, excerpted from Gustav Herling, *A World Apart,* trans. Andrzej Ciolkosz, pp. 86–96. Copyright 1951, © 1986 by Gustav Herling. Used by permission of Viking Penguin, a division of Penguin Group (USA), Inc., and of Andrew Nurnberg Associates International.

"Informers," by Lev Kopelev, excerpted from Lev Kopelev, *To Be Preserved Forever,* translated and edited by Anthony Austin, pp. 148–58. Copyright © 1975 by Ardis Publishers. English translation © 1977 by Anthony Austin. Reprinted by permission of HarperCollins Publishers. Editor's notes have been deleted or adapted.

"Jailers," by Lev Razgon, excerpted from Lev Razgon, *True Stories,* translated by John Crowfoot. Copyright © 1997 by Lev

Razgon, translation copyright © Ardis Publishers. Published in 1997 by Ardis Publishers/The Overlook Press. All rights reserved. www.overlookpress.com

"The Cooler," by Anatoly Marchenko, excerpted from Anatoly Marchenko, *My Testimony,* translated by Michael Scammel, pp. 64–71. Published by E. P. Dutton, New York, 1969.

"Liberation," by K. Petrus, excerpted from K. Petrus, *Uzniki Kommunizma,* originally published in 1996 by Izdatelstvo Im. Chekhova.

Soviet Culture and Power, by Katerina Clark and Evgeny Dobrenko, with Andrei Artizov and Oleg Naumov

The Soviet World of American Communism, by Harvey Klehr, John Earl Haynes, and Kyrill M. Anderson

Spain Betrayed: The Soviet Union in the Spanish Civil War, edited by Ronald Radosh, Mary R. Habeck, and G. N. Sevostianov

Stalinism as a Way of Life: A Narrative in Documents, edited by Lewis Siegelbaum and Andrei K. Sokolov

The Stalin-Kaganovich Correspondence, 1931–36, compiled and edited by R. W. Davies, Oleg V. Khlevniuk, E. A. Rees, Liudmila P. Kosheleva, and Larisa A. Rogovaya

Stalin's Letters to Molotov, 1925–1936, edited by Lars T. Lih, Oleg V. Naumov, and Oleg V. Khlevniuk

Stalin's Secret Pogrom: The Postwar Inquisition of the Soviet Jewish Anti-Fascist Committee, edited by Joshua Rubenstein and Vladimir P. Naumov

The Unknown Lenin: From the Secret Archive, edited by Richard Pipes

Voices of Revolution, 1917, by Mark D. Steinberg

The War Against the Peasantry, 1927–1930, edited by Lynne Viola, V. P. Danilov, N. A. Ivnitskii, and Denis Kozlov

JL